Tourism Crisis

And

REVIVAL

(In the Aftermath of Fall)

Dr. Chiranjib Kumar
PhD in Tourism & Hospitality Services
Professor – Author - Trainer
www.ckihmt.com

First Printed: Jun' 2020
(Kindle Books Publishing, USA)
www.amazon.com

ISBN: 9798657366990

ACKNOWLEDGEMENT

I would like to thank all those people who have not only supported me but also given motivation to complete my book on time. First of all I would like to express my gratitude to my students and their support without whom it was impossible to complete. I am deeply indebted to esteemed academics, authors, researchers and industry intellectuals for embarking with me on this book journey. Thank you for being my motivators and my source of inspiration. Your contributions, comments and insights have been of great value to me. Thank to those entire respondent who have not only responded to my query and questionnaires on time but also assisted in data collection process in their own way. A special thanks to Gambella University, Ethiopia for providing me sufficient time, resources and ideas to complete my book on time. This book would never been accomplished without cooperation from the publisher therefore, I am deeply indebted to my publisher for interest shown in publication. Finally my greatest thank to my parents and my lovely wife, you are just wonderful and a source of continuous inspiration and motivation.

PREFACE

The book basically unveils the secrets of Corona (Covid19) pandemic crisis through global trade war, tourism economics, and ancient wisdom of peace brotherhood and concept of universal acceptance routed through cooperation, non-violence and vital needs of people. The book explains about Corona crisis and opportunities in the aftermath of lockdown in conjugation with scapegoat marketing and falling cultural values which is very unique and need to be understood in order to revive the economy slowdown and developing trust among tourists, guests and hosts. The book describe about various approach of tourism planning; emerging tourism types; advantages and disadvantages as well.

Dr. Chiranjib Kumar
Author & Editor

ABBREVIATION

UNESCO- United Nations Educational Scientific and Cultural Organization

ICOMOS- International Council on Monuments and Sites

IUCN- International Union for Conservation of Nature

TIES- The International Ecotourism Society

CHAPTER No.   CONTENTS   PAGE NO.

1. **CORONA (covid-19) AND TOURISM: MOVING FORWARD IN THE AFTERMATH OF THE FALL**

2. **Corona (Covid-19) and Wildlife: Nature Finds Its Own Way For Treatment And Balancing**

3. **Organic Food Farming and Rural Tourism Development: An Opportunity To Restore The Happiness In The Aftermath of Covid-19 Pandemic**

4. **ECO-CULTURAL TOURISM AND CULTURAL HERITAGE MANAGEMENT IN THE ERA OF**

--@@--

- Tourism concept and practices and evolution of scapegoat marketing

- Explores the ideas of eco-cultural tourism, diaspora tourism, spiritual Odyssey tourism and organic farm tourism.

- Scope of nature based tourism leading to responsible tourism .

- Culture and wildlife Conservation as human integration and consciousness.

- Day driving to reduce the level of carbon emission in the air.

- Human need and level of product and designing through incorporating metaphysical need to satisfy the unlimited wants by redefining the need after lockdown and corona pandemic.

- Tourism economics, crisis and solutions for service sectors.

- Relationship Management in Marketing and importance of human touch for sustainable tourism development.

- Role of community based tourism and holistic marketing approach

- Neighbour tourism and regional tourism cooperation plan.

CHAPTER 1

CORONA (covid-19) AND TOURISM: MOVING FORWARD IN THE AFTERMATH OF THE FALL

Abstract

In recent years outbreak in diseases have devastated the emerging growth of tourism and development and has brought it down to minimum contribution to GDP. International tourism will have to face some complications in resurrection, but it doesn't mean that it has been collapsed totally. In such situations focus need to be given on domestic tourism and neighbour tourism. Tourism is, for the people, by the people and on the people like democracy. Hence it's never going to die. The article is based on opinions of and discussion with professionals.

Key Words: Corona, Covid19, Tourism, Virtual Tourism, Wildlife, Culture

1. Introduction

In recent years outbreak in diseases have devastated the emerging growth of tourism and development and has brought it down to minimum contribution to GDP. However this is due to one of the predetermined characteristics of tourism products that is " unstable demand" due to sudden occurrence of natural calamities or outbreak in diseases. No doubt in this that such uncontrollable disaster generates fear psychosis among tourist and visitors particularly international tourist who reach to tourism destinations after taking a lot of risks and spending a huge amount of money just for the sake of feeling " change" which is main reason behind tourism too. Dynamics of tourism will have both positive and negative impact and therefore "corona(covid19)" type of impacts should be taken as improving opportunity to overcome with challenges, and to bring dynamism in tourism.

International tourism will have to face some complications in resurrection, but it doesn't mean that it has been collapsed totally. In such situations focus need to be given on domestic tourism and neighbour tourism. Country like India, China, Ethiopia and Caribbean have tremendous potentials to resurrect through boosting the domestic tourists and motivating neighbouring countries through revenue sharing, data sharing, free visa and other trustworthy tools based on mutual sharing. Even European countries have similar advantages. Modernisation and globalisation have only good thing that it has power to erase the panic moments and dark side of life due availability of virtual technology (ICT- Information Communication Technology) and big social networking space.

2. **The major challenges** that tourism industry seems to be faced due to impact on other sectors would be,

I)   Economic Slowdown

II) Job loss in tourism & non tourism sectors

III) Trust for host countries /destinations

IV) Trust and faith in guest/tourists/travellers

V) Strict norms for travellers

VI) Rigid Government policies

VII) Social Distancing instead of physical distancing

3. **Potential opportunities** could be in following areas,

I) Agri-tourism

II) Rural Tourism

III) Tribal Tourism

IV) Nature Based Tourism

V) Cruiseship Tourism

VI) Wildlife Tourism

VII) Birds Watching

VIII) Organic Farm Tourism

IX) Forest Coffee Tourism

X) Livestock Tourism

XI)   Spiritual Odyssey Tourism

XII)   Corona Tourism

Destinations affected by Covid-19 outbreak would have potential to be emerged as corona tourism like terror tourism in future. Even doomsday tourism and dark tourism can't be ignored due to the lost of life of many people in different countries other than country of origin.

The future of tourism would more or less inclined towards nature based tourism, Agri-tourism and Tribal Tourism activities. Even scope of wildlife Tourism, birds watching and adventure tourism can not be denied.

It is confirmed that now tourists would take lessons through covid-19 like pandemic and will plan their future tourism destinations or activities on the basis of physical distancing and also distance of tourism products from crowd (human populations), air and sound pollution. The people would develop more faith in indigenous lifestyle and idea of staying in tranquility rather than disturbances which would further led the foundation of nature based tourism and Tribal (ethnic) / indigenous Tourism. People relations with nature will come more closure and distance from big malls and other manmade attractions will increase.

4. **Virtual Tourism:** it could emerge as stimulator of tourism for time being to generate awareness regarding nature, culture, wildlife, craft, food and environment conservation by motivating to take ecotourism or responsible tourism to save the earth, nature and culture.

5. The Way Forward

The growth and development of tourism totally depends of "change" and it for sure that in coming days also people would be in need of " change" from place of residence. Man is a social animal hence keeping always in lockdown condition would not be possible for human beings.

Teasers and trailers of future marketing should be more oriented to tribals, nature and their culture. And connect other typology of tourism with tribal, nature and indigenous culture in responsible ways to grab opportunities from market by building trust in terms of safety and attractions.

Tourists have lost the trust and faith in visiting countries and in same manner communities of host countries also lost trust in tourist/guest/visitors that need to be redirected. The main reason behinds this is dirty global politics and political structure in some countries which suppress the freedom of speech. Socio-economic structure in such countries is partially or completely not allowing native communities to speak out for the cause. On the other hand tourists and travellers have also become irresponsible towards their attitude to protect host communities and cooperate in following travel formalities.

Therefore the important exit and entry points of any tourist destinations must have proper scanning, checking and verification facilities, particularly at airports. One loose connection may result in devastations again.

The most important step would be if the concerned government could impose some hard restrictions of consumption of particularly type of food and beverage for native communities as well as visitors to the areas. But it should be done on regular basis involving both local community and research scholars.

Tourism is, for the people, by the people and on the people like democracy. Hence it's never going to die. It has been since time immemorial and would be remained until the existence of this fast moving world. Tourism is happy religion of the world which consists of joy, happiness, tranquility, recreation, adventure and pleasure through learning from guest to host settings and vise-versa.

The glory of tourism would bring back the derailed smiling faces to serve the world again to earn blessings and generate pleasure.

6. Limitations

Any generalized idea is not right due to variations in size, goal, changing perceptions and region and literatures followed.

7. Direction to further research

The further research must direct itself for conducting such investigations. This will make the study more meaningful to find linkage more effectively.

References

https://www.who.int/emergencies/diseases/novel-coronavirus-2019

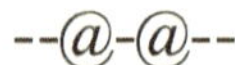

(Page purposely kept blank)

CHAPTER 2

Corona (Covid-19) and Wildlife: Nature Finds Its Own Way For Treatment And Balancing

Abstract

Nature is divine. Many times it has provided opportunity of improvement to the people, but due to high ambition people ignored it. Successors have crossed their limit over predecessors and started interfering in the peaceful habitat of wildlife. The nature has found its own way to regulate it. The article tried to focus on emerging pattern of natural balancing through covid-19 concept based on literature review.

Key Words: balancing, corona(covid-19), ecology, God, nature, truth, wildlife

1. Introduction

Corona(Covid-19) virus has been trying to engulf the whole world leaving aside the wildlife and marine life and raised several questions for human beings.

Q. Have we ever thought about consequences of unwise decisions?

Q. Do we have super natural power to control the natural disasters?

Q. Do we seek of " who bothers?" like mentality?

These are some critical questions that every human being should answer.

Nature has its own rules and regulations to control the excessive amount of pollution and encroachment. In last four decades human dominancy to control the nature and scarce resources has been increased to multiple times in unlawful ways. The exploitation against nature and damage to ecological balance has developed tendency of selfishness among human beings which forced the divine nature to take harsh decisions in the form of Covid-19 to punish the human beings for their misdeeds.

People by heart never considered nature as "God" (truth) who created this beautiful world instead kept on wandering in search of manmade cultural God. Even cultural God also instructed the man to follow the nature and its rule. But who cares? Man is most dangerous animal on this earth. He will keep on hunting without caring nature and ecology, because of fear of not getting food for self and family and unlimited wants.

The question is "why?".

The answer lies in question itself. Man is selfish and therefore he could not accept the regime of nature(real truth). It is said "truth prevails" and due to this nature becomes one barrier on the way of vanity.

Recently many news and articles have tried to focus on the improving ecosystem of marine life, terrestrial life and air quality of some densely populated areas of the earth. Because of Corona pandemic and lockdown, many cities, towns, tourist destinations, recreation sites such as beaches, riverside and forests, are free from noise and irresponsible activities.

Wildlife and marine life, both have been found enjoying their life freely without much disturbances. Some migratory birds have been seen returning to their old destinations after two hundred years in England.

2. Corona Virus (Covid-19)

COVID-19 is the infectious disease caused by the most recently discovered coronavirus. This new virus and disease were unknown before the outbreak began in Wuhan, China, in December 2019 (WHO'2020). Million of people have been infected across the world and thousands of death have been occurred due covid-19 pandemic. It is one of the drastic reaction of nature as per Newton's third law.

3. Literature Review

There were number of articles which have focused on the covid-19 and discussed about long term impacts on wildlife. But most of them have concentrated on the positive impact of outbreak in corona(covid-19) viral disease.

Paul J.,et.al(2020), White-tailed eagles not seen in England for over 240 years have been spotted on the North York Moors after making a remarkable 300-mile trip.The bird, also known as the fish eagle, is the UK's largest bird of prey with a wingspan of up to 2.5 metres. It became extinct here early in the 20th century due to illegal killing.Forestry England and the Roy Dennis Wildlife Foundation are leading a project to reintroduce them, releasing a group on the Isle of Wight last year. They are GPS tracking four young birds making their first big trips. They mostly eat fish but also take birds, rabbits and hares.

Dan, B.(2020) the Coronavirus pandemic, and the consequent blocking of activities that has been implemented in many countries around the world, continue to have positive effects on nature, animals and the air we breathe. It seems that this dramatic situation has brought, in the midst of so many sufferings and deprivations, also a period of "breathing" and well-being to the planet that hosts us and to so many creatures that are often threatened by the presence of man. In eastern India, what has not been seen for a long time has happened along the coast of the state of Odisha. Sea turtles, animals notoriously vulnerable and threatened by pollution and human activities, took advantage of the quarantine to take back their spaces without being disturbed. Hundreds of thousands of olive tortoises (Olive Ridley, or Lepidochelys olivacea) who managed to reach the shore, on the beach of Rushikulya, to make their nests and lay their eggs. Everything happened in a safer and more protected way than the normal situation in which man, with his fishing and tourism activities, would certainly have disturbed this fascinating natural process. In general, in fact, such an event would attract crowds of tourists eager to attend, with obvious disturbance to the turtles. Besides, there often are the acts of poaching: unscrupulous people stealing eggs from the beach and then reselling them in local markets. This year the splendid sea turtles were able to nest in complete tranquility. Really good news for these animals, that hadn't even landed on Rushikulya beach last year. Nature, with man's less present, is winning the battle. Don't you think this should always be guaranteed to it?

Dan, C. et.al(2020), wildlife is used globally on a daily basis, from medicinal plants and edible fungi, to wild meat in Europe, North America, Southern Africa and elsewhere. Wildlife trade enables people in many parts of the world to meet their basic needs and can provide livelihood benefits from harvesting or farming. The pandemic has led to some wildlife conservation organisations to call for blanket bans on wildlife trade on public health grounds. They include bans on commercial trade in wildlife for human consumption and the closure of these markets. More extreme calls from more than 200 organisations include ending the keeping, breeding, domestication and use of all wildlife, which also covers traditional medicine.

Eric, R. (2020), The role of biodiversity in disease prevention has received increased attention of late. In a 2015 "state of knowledge review" of biodiversity and human health by the United Nations, scientists wrote that "an ecological approach to disease, rather than a simplistic 'one germ, one disease' approach, will provide a richer understanding of disease-related outcomes." Recent research has given more support to the idea that biodiversity protection in one part of the world can prevent novel diseases from emerging and leaping into another.

Lee, H. (Bloomberg'2020), there are four critical facets of pandemic prevention, according to Lee Hannah, senior scientist at Conservation International. Three of them make immediate sense against the backdrop of our current emergency: stockpile masks and respirators; have testing infrastructure ready; and ban the global wildlife trade, including the open animal markets where COVID-19 may have first infected people. His fourth recommendation is more grandiose: "Take care of nature."

Richard, O.(2020), a disease ecologist at the Cary Institute of Ecosystem Studies. According to him "We are messing with natural systems in certain ways that can make them much more dangerous than they would otherwise be,", a. "And biodiversity loss is one of those. Climate change is another."

Katherine, G.(2020), Finding the source of this virus will help ensure that another outbreak of this magnitude does not happen again, and many experts are investigating wildlife exploitation as a possible cause.There are also a number of experts who suggest that humanity's destruction of animal habitats is partly to blame. Back in 2008, a team led by chair of ecology and biodiversity at UCL Kate Jones found that 60% of the 335 diseases identified between 1960 and 2004 came from animals. Jones linked these zoonotic diseases to both environmental changes and human behaviors. Ecological disruption, urbanization and population growth were all driving factors bringing humans and livestock closer and closer to the types of wild animals that they had never been exposed to before.

Katie, W.(the conservation'2020), The current available evidence indicates COVID-19 was first transmitted in a wildlife market in Wuhan. The disease likely originated in pangolins, bats, or a combination of both and was then transmitted to humans.While various commentators have blamed pangolins, bats, or even our lack of "mastery" of wildlife, the real cause of this pandemic goes deeper—into the laws, cultures and institutions of most countries. At the root of the problem is a social phenomenon called "human-wildlife conflict." This is when the interests of humans and the needs of wildlife overlap in a negative way. Both the illegal wildlife trade and zoonotic diseases (that is, diseases transmitted from animals to humans) are aspects of human-wildlife conflict. This ubiquitous phenomenon is poorly addressed in both international and domestic laws. And this grave omission has led to disastrous effects on humanity, as COVID-19 has shown.

Many researchers say the coronavirus pandemic underscores the need for a more holistic "one health" approach, which views human, animal and environmental health as interconnected. "There needs to be a cultural shift from a community level up about how we treat animals, our understanding of the dangers and biosecurity risks that we're exposing ourselves to," said Kate Jones, chair of ecology and biodiversity at University College London. "That means leaving ecosystems intact, not destroying them. It means thinking in a more long-term way." The next pandemic is already coming, unless humans change how we interact with wildlife.

"Pandemics as a whole are increasing in frequency," said Peter Daszak, a disease ecologist who is president of Eco Health

Alliance, a public health organization that studies emerging diseases. "It's not a random act of God. It's caused by what we do to the environment. Bats have a superhero-like immune system that allows them to become "reservoirs to many pathogens that do not impact them but can have a tremendous impact on us if they're able to make the jump," said Thomas Gillespie, a disease ecologist at Emory University.

Shannon Schaller, the Senior Wildlife Biologist for CPW(Colorado Parks and Wildlife) northeast region said that essentially if a park, trail or open space is crowded with people, wildlife will go to a different area that is more quiet. Likewise, if an urban park or open space that used to be very busy is suddenly quiet, and it can provide food, water or shelter, then more and more wildlife will likely start utilizing the area. "As we slow down or even eliminate our activity in certain areas and they feel the comfort of being able to hunt, eat or rest because we are not there, that's logical".

Helen, B,(The Environmental,BBC'2020), Feasting on exotic game has become a sign of status and wealth in some Asian countries. The desire for wildlife as food or medicine drives a trade in wild animals, some procured illegally, creating a breeding ground for disease and the chance for viruses to leap to humans. All eyes, therefore, are on the soon-to-be amended wildlife protection law - whether and how it would address those loopholes. Prof Dirk Pfeiffer of City University of Hong Kong says the real issue is demand. "The people who are providing them, whether that's farmed wild animals or animals from the wild, that's an important source of income for them. Pushing it underground, that's not the solution, so it needs to be a phased process." Prof Cunningham says if we're to stop another pandemic in the future, we must focus on causes as well as effects. At the root of the problem is the destruction of nature, bringing animals and humans into conflict. "Even in protected forests, the forests are still there, but the wildlife's gone from within them because they have ended up in markets," he says. ".And it's easy to finger point, but it's not just happening in China, it's happening in many other countries and even in the western world.

4. Challenges

I)   Man- arrogant nature and vanity.

II)   Dependency on wildlife trade as livelihood option.

III)   Cultural barrier particularly in terms of ethnic food and indigenous method of treatment to a disease

IV)   Urbanisation due to global trade and shifting patterns.

V)   International politics

VI)   Desire for luxurious life and dominancy.

VII)   Lack of coordination

VIII)   Poaching and poverty

5. Opportunities

a) Responsible Wildlife Tourism and Nature based tourism

b) Ecotourism and eco-cultural tourism

c) Holistic and sustainable development

d) Nature and wildlife conservation from primary class

e) Agri-tourism and alternate business model in village

f) Rigid rules and regulations for global wildlife trade

g) Nature and wildlife conservation Laws and obligations

h) Indigenous knowledge transfer and proper monitoring at local level

i) Participatory Forest Management and Developing Environmental Calendar to facilitate both Farming and non-farming activity.

j) Cooperative based occupational framework for local people to control, monitor and increasing employment.

6. Conclusion

The new corona(covid-19) virus has emerged from the global wildlife trade and would might be able to end the global wildlife trade. It has taught a big lesson to the inhabitants of the earth and advise to control the high ambitions and give honour to the nature. Wildlife have also been given right to exist with full freedom by nature. They should not be treated as food and raw material of producing luxurious items for men. Playing dirty politics around wildlife and blaming each-other for natural calamities and disruptive ecological balance would not help in long term survival.

Government should develop listening ability and must listen to the voice of ecologists, biologists, naturalist, explorers and other conservationist. In hospitality " delay means denied", so suggestions, recommendations and policies need to be implemented on time to avoid any negative impact. Indigenous knowledge transfer is must to save the culture but it should be done in controlled way. Regular counselling of local community would be helpful in achieving the aim of wildlife conservation and natural harmony. Assuming solidarity in this fast moving globalised world is like fooling to yourself. But this world is interconnected. Experience this connectivity. This is the true world wide web (www). Any thought word, action by any one of us has an impact to the totality of universe. As for the law of transformation of energy, the sum total of energy in the universe is constant. It can neither be created nor destroyed and it can only be transformed from one state to another. This applies to all our thoughts, all our words and actions. Save nature and wildlife to safeguard yourself from landing into unwanted disasters.

7. Limitations

Any generalized idea is not right due to variations in size, goal, changing perceptions and region and literatures followed.

8. Direction to further research

The further research must direct itself for conducting such investigations. This will make the study more meaningful to find linkage more effectively.

9. Acknowledgement

The researcher would like to extend their gratitude to all the respondents, professor, scholars, authors, scientists, biologists, ecologists, wildlife professionals and news reporters of various organizations. And finally to Research Directorate of University for providing sufficient time and resources.

10.   Reference

- Kumar, C K., 2017, Ethiopian orthodox Christianity and Indian Jain philosophy: A common interlinkage perspective of cultural conservation and peace building in the world, International Conference, Makelle University, Ethiopia.

- https://www.msn.com/en-in/news/world/white-tailed-eagles-with-25metre-wingspan-return-to-england-after-240-years/ar-BB12madK?ocid=sf/04-2020

- https://fun-owl.com/while-india-is-on-quarantine-thousands-of-undisturbed-sea-turtles-estimate-60-million-eggs/03-2020

- https://phys.org/news/2020-04-coronavirus-blanket-wildlife-response.amp

- https://time.com/5817363/wildlife-habitats-disease-pandemics/04-2020

- https://inhabitat.com/the-connection-between-covid-19-and-wildlife-exploitation/04-2020

- https://phys.org/news/2020-04-laws-human-wildlife-conflictthis-vulnerable-pandemics.amp

- https://www.washingtonpost.com/science/2020/04/03/coronavirus-wildlife-environment/?outputType=amp

- https://denver.cbslocal.com/2020/04/03/wildlife-behavior-during-coronavirus-shutdown/amp/

- https://sports.yahoo.com/amphtml/coronavirus-putting-spotlight-global-wildlife-232656211.html

- https://www.who.int/news-room/q-a-detail/q-a-coronaviruses

- Raghavendra,S.http://hinduismprimer.blogspot.co.uk/2013/03/make-ifference.html/

(page purposely kept blank)

CHAPTER 3

Organic Food Farming and Rural Tourism Development: An Opportunity To Restore The Happiness In The Aftermath of Covid-19 Pandemic

Abstract

Organic food farming and rural tourism has been emerged as an impressive niche concept in recent days. It contributes a real happiness in the life of humans and other species. Some of the corporate houses have shown a deep interest in organizing MICE (Meeting, Incentive, Conference/Convention and Exposition/Exhibition/Events) into rural areas. Common people are almost frustrated with hybrid food products and polluted environment in surrounding and Corona(covid19) like pandemic has already engulfed thousands of people and infected millions. Therefore, they are big market for organic food and rural tourism. These people can be motivated to enjoy weekends in nearby rural destination. Few generations ago, in the 1930's, approximately 45% of Americans lived on farms. This demographic gradually but steadily declined as people migrated to urban centers, and over time, to suburbs. Today, people who claim farming as their principal occupation has come down to minimal and the same period of time the US population has more than doubled, and demand for agricultural products has increased accordingly. The country like Ethiopia and India have already developed organic farms and most of the farmers are involved in organic type of farming. Sikkim a state of India has done tremendous in organic food farming. The present paper focuses on changing dimension of tourism and its sustainable approach. It emphasized on bringing people and corporate both to nature to avail its originalities. It also focuses on mutual benefits of farming(agricultural) and non-farming activities(tourism) . It also focus on Corona (covid19) pandemic which is a result of concentrated growth of town and shifting patterns of people.

New venture need to be created on the basis of suggested framework and model. Land using and settlement pattern should be mapped to develop rural tourism activities.

Keyword: corona(covid19), Farm tourism, Organic food, MICE, Rural tourism, Venture, Micro financer

1. Introduction

Food, Farm and Tourism (FFT) are closely interlinked. Food is an important and essential need of human beings which provides ultimate satisfaction in the process of tourism. And these foods come from farms which are managed by farmers in rural areas. In the process of tourism, a tourist also consume food. It is said "health is wealth" but what happens when you get spoiled, altered and more hybrid food at your home or tourism destinations. Altered and spoiled food results in bad health and serious ailments. Organic food, fresh from farm is the option which a tourist could look for to avoid health hazards. Breathing in fresh air of green farm will not only improve the health condition of tourist/visitors but also help farmers to survive in mutual way.

Organic food and tourism has now become the need of fast moving globalized world where Corona (covid19) like pandemic have devastated the economy of different nations due to lockdown and pushed them into the economic recession. Corona(covid19) disease has taken a catastrophe shape and has killed thousands of people around the different corners in the world. Scientists have started speaking about the requirement of sound immune system in the body. Food is an important part of getting proper nutrients in the body and hence deserves vital attention to develop proper immune system in the body. Organic farming is the solution for it. From individual to corporate houses are looking for organic food in their meals and willing to visit the new places, full of natural attraction, scenic beauty and tranquility and for enjoying change too. Many destinations in India and even different parts of world have been emerged as MICE destination. Everyone wants some change and a day leave from regular routines life style to enjoy the peace of mind with pleasure. Sub-urban destination and resort has been taking benefits of MICE activities done by corporates.

The following were specific aim of this paper

1.1. Aim and Objectives

- to generate awareness regarding organic food and farm tourism.

- to explore the other possibility of rural tourism and entrepreneurship ability in farmers.

- to take on tourism as farm and non-farm activities for the betterment of farmers in rural areas.

- to suggest a framework for farmer and corporate for taking mutual benefits of tourism activities.

1.2. Research Methodology

The research methodology is based on literatures reviews, opinions drawn during discussion and observation. The paper is reflective in nature.

1.3. Research question

1.3.1.Q. How corporate world could contribute to rural tourism development?

1.3.2.Q. How to motivate urban people to take on village trip and motivate farmers to cultivate organic food?

1.4. Rural tourism and entrepreneurship ability through Agri-tourism

Rural people can be prepared for organic farming as it will not only boost their economic condition but also entrepreneurial ability to face the challenges of this competitive world. It will bring tourist to their farm as a part of farm or rural tourism and would also motivate to buy their organic products directly from their farm. This also creates a framework of interdependency where several buyers, suppliers and ultimately consumers would be in the value chain. Large size hotels particularly ecotels (eco-friendly hotels) will definitely try to get benefits through networking. This will further boost the morale and confidence of a large number of farmers in rural area to become an entrepreneur by connecting them into various tourism organizations and hotels. Retailers and big malls are already interested in selling organic products. And they have been selling it for the last ten years in India and other parts of the world.

Big corporate houses, tourism agencies and renowned hotel companies may enter into a memorandum of understanding (MoU) with rural farmers for taking mutual benefits through rural tourism, agri-tourism and organic farming. Companies must provide resources to farmer for non-farm activities in conjugation with regular farm activities. Motivating farmers to take on tourism related activities for their benefits will not only increase their revenue earnings potential, but also add a varied skill in them in the form of tourism and hospitality.

Many Indian farmers are currently involved in or are considering the use of agri-tourism and farm tourism as means of diversifying their farm operation. The impact of tourism on rural area and particularly on woman in India can't be ignored and neglected. The best example of woman entrepreneur development and evolvement of other micro entrepreneurs ability could be seen in the state of

Gujarat (India) where in villages of "Kutchh" all the village persons have involved themselves in the business of tourism and have created a role model for policy makers and practitioners. It has given a tremendous effect on the life style and has become a part of their livings. Tourism and tourist both of them have influenced and motivated the rural people to become as micro entrepreneurs through the promotion of their art-craft, cuisines, fairs, festivals, and green organic farms.

Village is a unit of national integration and world formation in which economy grow and survive. Therefore special attention should be given to the rural economy development and new venture creation, as it is foundation of existence of any human beings of this fast moving world. It also provides basic needs for livelihood like food in direct way and materials for cloths and shelters in indirect form. Village gives birth to sub-urban, urban and metropolitan cities and provides necessary supplies to industries and people for growth, development and their livelihood too. One should never forget the drawbacks of new shifting patterns of people from rural area to urban area due to one sided growth and development, particularly in developing country like India and also developed country like USA, UK which has suffered a lot and still struggling to overcome with economy slow down and growing number of unemployed youth as a result of blind growth. The present global recession, economic slowdown and corona(covid-19) pandemic is all due to ignoring nature and neglecting of rural people and their demand. A time will come when people would be dying due to high inflation due to insufficient supply of food items and raw materials from village. Therefore, to overcome with economy slow down and corona virus like pandemics, government of every nation should try their level best to stop shifting of rural people to urban by providing and developing sufficient amenities, resources, infrastructures, super structures, primary to technical education in rural area itself. And also motivate them to farm in organic way by providing subsidy on agricultural equipments and seeds.

1.5. Land reform and acquisition process

Many countries have been talking about the land reforms and acquisition bill and facing difficulties in passing it through parliament and legislature assembly. Every political party is mad about it and corporate houses have been watching it with greedy eyes. Rural Tourism can play a vital role in connecting farmers with corporates to facilitate hazel free business option through memorandum of understanding (MoU).

1.6. Organic Food and Farm Tourism

Production of organic vegetables, fruits and other crops are really a very tough and expensive tasks. But still country like India and Ethiopia has been doing it since a long time, knowingly or unknowingly. It has preserved the indigenous method of farming and animal husbandry to some extent. Starting from some vegetable to small egg, country chicken and other meat products and even milk are organic.

Starting from crops to grains and other commodities should be totally free from all types pesticide residues. In order to grow them, the first step is soil sanitation. Soil should be made free from pesticides. It is a long process. The water used for cultivation should be free from pesticides. When pesticides are sprayed in the neighbors field, they may get drifted and contaminate to connected field. Hence, organic food cannot be grown in small patches of land. The only thing is that they may not be spraying pesticides directly.

A global issue in rural tourism is the need to balance resource conservation with development, especially because it is clear that rural tourism depends on a special ambience and access to natural environment. Native people are acutely aware of the need for both cultural and landscape conservation. Unfortunately in many countries it seems likely that environmental standards and development regulations are inadequate to fully protect rural areas and communities from the potential negative impacts of unregulated or mass tourism. Specific risk include disruption of community life. Many rural tourism families decide to add a tourism enterprise to their existing agricultural activities. This might be done to supplement farm income, or perhaps for lifestyle reasons such as meeting new people. Retirement opportunity can also be seen as motivating factor towards organic farming and rural tourism(Stephen P, Donald Getz,1997)

Niels C. Nielsen, Marie-Kathrine Aae Nissen and F. Just, 2010, has focused on development potential for farm wanting to diversify their business, and their possibilities for economic support.

Carol K, David C, Yu-Fai Leung and Stacy Sanders, 2007, wishing to engage in sustainable tourism by providing resources that can help them to succeed. As any new ag-related product appears on the horizon, it is their responsibility to explore, evaluate, and educate about the product. In this regard, tourism is no different from a new variety of seed corn.

1.7. Findings

Organic crops are more resilient than conventionally grown and GM crops

Organic corn yields were 31 per cent higher than conventional yields in years of drought. These drought yields are remarkable when compared to genetically modified (GM) "drought tolerant" varieties, which showed increases of only 6.7 per cent to 13.3 per cent over conventional (non-drought resistant) varieties.

The effects of climate change bring more uncertainty to farming, with increased drought predicted for some parts of the country. It has become obvious that weather patterns are changing, and looking to the future, food crops will need the resilience to adapt.

Organic farming is more efficient than conventional farming

Conventional agriculture requires large amounts of oil to produce, transport and apply fertilizers and pesticides. Nitrogen fertilizer is the single biggest energy cost for conventional farming, representing 41% of overall energy costs. Organic systems used 45% less energy overall than conventional systems. Production efficiency was 28% higher in the organic systems, with the conventional no-till system being the least efficient in terms of energy usage.

The extra energy required for fertilizer production and farm fuel use in conventional systems also contributes to greenhouse gas emissions (GHG). Conventional systems emit almost 40% more GHG per pound of crop production in comparison to the organic systems.

According to the Environmental Working Group and soil scientists at Iowa State University, America's "Corn Belt" is losing precious topsoil up to 12 times faster than government estimates.

Organic farming creates more jobs

Industrial agriculture has replaced human hands with machines and chemical inputs. According to the EPA, in the last century agricultural labor efficiency increased from 27.5 acres/worker to 740 acres/worker. Joel Salatin, organic farmer and author of best-selling books on sustainable farming, views these statistics as another reason for us to return to our farming roots. "People say our system can't feed the world, but they're absolutely wrong," he says, "Yes, it will take more hands, but we've got plenty of them around."

Our current food production system is in need of repair. We need to promote organic systems which respect the integrity of soil health and sustainable systems. Until recently it was thought that our national and global food needs were too big to be met with natural, organic food production systems. Recent studies confirm, however, that organic farming is the way of the future. We need, both collectively and as individuals, to support the organic food movement to enable the process to move forward with the research, seed development and farming practices needed to feed a hungry world (Greg Seaman' 2011) .

1.8.Suggestive Framework for Organic Rural Tourism Development

Venture creation with different stakeholders can be the best option in regard to organic food and rural tourism development. Venture can be defined as a project or activity which is new, exciting, and difficult because it involves the risk of failures but at the same time it brings large profits if it becomes successful. But it can also be defined in different way, which may be in context of non-profit making tie-ups, collaboration, partnering, and affiliation as a compulsory part of taking CSR to promote peace, prosperity and awareness in some unidentified or identified zones. Venture can also be created for providing training and skill development to give out the best to local communities to safeguard the interest of their own keeping in view future consequences of underdeveloped, backward or undeveloped areas in the form of terrorism, robbery and theft around the growing business. It also helps in meeting with the antisocial activities that may create a big problem in future due to rising poverty and unemployment.

Therefore venture is one type of assistance or help that may be extended to any person, region, state or countries to establish self-dependency. Some common types of venture in context of rural economy development through tourism could be the followings,

(i) **Microfinance ventures:** Micro financers are the financer who is having capacity to finance someone after meeting with their daily expenses and also have sufficient fund to spend on charity, donations and social work. There are person who spent a lot of money in the form of donations in temples or orphanage for getting internal satisfaction or event for maintaining their external status.

Now such type of people may be motivated through various means to re-direct their donation to some realist world. Instead of paying money to a temple authority in the form of donation, same to be invested in rural areas on any development head. Even such type of micro financer may spent whole amount of pre-decided donation to train and develop rural people to become a organic farmer and tourism micro entrepreneur of their craft/skill. And in lieu of assistance provided by financer the borrower should return a part of that amount to him so that he/she can further help others. Government should also come forward to help such type of micro financer through tax holiday policy on such type of invested money. Government authority should launch such type of things in a campaign form. This way more and more people will come to join the campaign and the economy of rural or backward area would become strong.

(ii) **Partnering with NGOs:** NGO (Non-Governmental Organization) may play an important role by generating social awareness regarding Organic tourism business and govt. policies. NGO should come forward to form a welfare trust to help the needy person, village or micro entrepreneurs.

(iii) **Tie-up with Big Companies/Corporate Houses:** Village Authority (Gram Panchayat) should directly approach to big companies for taking new initiatives in the direction of eco-friendly venture creation. They should highlight there organic farms and other potentials, skills, art and craft, cuisines, culture, folk dance, folklores, fairs & festivals, ceremonies & traditions as well as other natural resources for getting more benefits out of it.

(iv) Collaboration with Foreign Banks & Financial Institution: if possible then personnel of foreign banks and financial institution should be called to check the progress report of village and farms in physical way for getting more financial assistance.

(v) Membership & Affiliations of Relevant Organizations: for getting opportunity to speak out the failures, problems, and successes through one common platform and to safeguard the interest of farming and tourism. To gain popularity and recognition on country level as well as world level.

(vi) Media Partner: media plays a very effective role in promoting any events or destination in attractive way. Therefore media personality should be called for capturing the evolving activities of village as well as its tourism potentiality. There are people in the world who just come for shopping or eating and even for buying an item which he/she has seen on TV. Magazines, news paper.

(vii) Tourist- Host venture: to promote a new kind of tourism, in this process ―Give Back and Getaway Tourism (GBGT)‖ would be perhaps the best option to involve guest/visitors/tourists in the improvement process of host community's livelihood. This type of venture may be created on short term or day basis.

1.8.2.   Rotational   Entrepreneurial Framework-The best suitable framework would be to start a micro enterprise have sufficient land for farming and involving maximum people of common interests and allotting a designation on the basis of their share value, skills, or previous experiences. Certain points should be allotted to each and every individual working in enterprise for revenue sharing at the end of every month as a part of their salary or income. Promotion or increase in income should be based on total reward points collected by the concerned workers in a enterprises through holding the position. If anyone achieved the highest point which is required to become an entrepreneurs then he/she should be provided assistance for his/her new organic farm through new venture creation. And this way cycle of becoming farm micro entrepreneurs should be continued by the help of concerned government or big corporate houses.

The causes of poverty and of environmental degradation are inter-related, suggesting that, approaching sustainable development requires understanding the issues from many angles, not just say an environmentalist or economics perspective alone. The systematic framework should be developed in such a way so that it could give maximum benefits to all the villages near to it i.e. proximity of 02 km of radius. Motivating factors need to be developed among all the participant i.e. different farmers and tribes who came a long way from their village to attend the induction or farm visit. After getting motivation and inspiration from the people hosting the visits in organic farm they can also implement the same strategies, plan and structure to accomplish their objectives and could earn maximum from it for their better livelihood.

1.9. Conclusion

Organic food is at maximum demand, whereas **organic rural tourism** is still untapped area of tourism. It can be promoted as the potential tourism product in rural areas to attract food lover, urban people, corporate and other agrarians, particularly ecotels, green hotels, and other segments of ecolodging providers who are looking for organic foods and farms. The other market segment can be an organic wine manufacturer, organic juice manufacturer, malls, stores and others prospective customers.

Farmers can also be targeted as visitors of these farms for induction and training. Human beings are made up of almost organic elements and therefore we can say for existence in long run "organic body require, organic food" and " rural tourism requires organic farm". It was also believed that the regional imbalances that were a historical legacy of the colonial pattern of development could be redressed by tourism, since the resources required for tourism were -gifts of nature. Through the development of tourism backward areas as well as undeveloped areas could be integrated into the level of development of the advanced areas. Globalization has put certain pressure on the Economy, where the backward and less developed regions have often paid the price of the new system particularly rural economy.

New venture need to be created on the basis of suggested framework and model. Government and NTOs(National Tourism Organisation) have to play a leading role to bring all the stakeholders in the tourism process together and to see that sustainable development ensure a distribution of benefits and costs.

Land using and settlement pattern should be mapped to develop tourism activities. Tourism is happy industry and a kind of new religion of this fast moving word that has eradicated inequalities, barrier of castes, cultures, and religion from society and has generated peace, prosperity and consensus in different zones. Therefore, it could become one of the best powerful boosters of rural economy and nation as well. Rural tourism, Agri-tourism and Farm tourism through organic food cultivation would bring sustainable development and ecological balance. The only solution to pandemic like Corona(covid19) is to return back to organic food farming and rural tourism. Avoid eating hybrid food items and dedicate your time for nature conservation.

1.10. Limitations and direction of further research

The present paper is based on only limited number of literatures review, observation during trips to few farms and experience gained through journey. Further it can be taken more seriously on wider perspective for future research.

Reference

- Carol K, David C, Yu-Fai Leung and Stacy Sanders, 2007, Sustainable farm tourism: Understanding and Managing Environmental Impacts of Visitor Activities, Journal of Extension, Vol-45,No.2

- Chiranjib K, Aditi C., Kushrestha S., 2011, Rural Economic Development and New Venture Creation Opportunities through Tourism Business, ICER-BRIC International Conference, Indian Institute of Management Bangalore, IIMBBRIC015, pg. 21-24

- Greg Seaman, 2011, Sustainable, organic farming practices are the best way to feed the future.

- https://www.who.int/emergencies/diseases/novel-coronavirus-2019

- https://tourismjournals.asia/Articles-/-Insight/corona(covid-19) And Tourism/04-2020

- Kumar Chiranjib, 03/2020, Corona(covid-19) and Tourism: Moving Forward In The Aftermath of The Fall, Academia.edu, Articles/Research note

- Niels Chr. Nielsen, Marie-Kathrine Aae Nissen and F. Just, 2010, Rural tourism-return to the farm perspective, 19th Nordic Symposium in Tourism and Hospitality Research, Danish centre for rural research, University of southern Denmark.

- Stephen P, Donald Getz,1997, The Business of rural tourism: international perspective, International Thomson Business Press USA,Pg. 198-199

- www.agritourism.in/tourism-in-India.html retrieved on 27/04/2015

- www.incredibleindia.org/en/trade-product/products/rural-tourism/about-the-product retrieved on 27th April2015

Further Reading (Book)

- Chiranjib kumar, 2017, Ecotourism Dynamics: Perspective of Culture, Wildlife and Other Dimensions, CreateSpace Publication, USA, Amazon.com

(page purposely kept blank)

CHAPTER 4

Cultural Conservation In The Era Of Globalisation And Commodofication: An Opportunity Through Eco-Cultural Tourism

ABSTRACT

The word culture and heritage have become an integral part for many countries in the world as these countries have already started feeling the threats in terms of degradation in cultural values and tradition because of globalization of trade and tourism. The impact of globalization and migration on native culture can be seen easily in the state. The article focuses on the importance of conservation and preservation of culture in conjugation with eco-cultural tourism. The paper has tried to analyze the data collected through review of literature and opinions of authors, scholars and culture bureau officials. The focus group discussion was also conducted to support the data and finally providing the framework and direction to further research in regard to cultural tourism planning and heritage management. The study not only conclude tourism as major challenge in regards to planning, conservation, and management of culture and heritage, but also considered it as main economic booster and conservation agent particularly eco-cultural tourism.

Key Words : commodification, conservation, cultural planning, eco-cultural tourism, globalisation, heritage

INTRODUCTION

Culture has always given the new dimensions to human beings and tourism has provided platform to all such type of ancient culture for growth and development through its various form considering the harmonial relationship in between tourist and hosts. Where tourism has contributed in globalization of cultures, there culture has worked as main booster and element of tourism phenomenon. Cultural tourism satisfies the need of curiosity of tourists, that involves visiting to cultural places, historical monuments, and religious places of cultural importance. 'Eco-cultural tourism promotes learning and awareness regarding conservation of indigenous cultural heritage and its various dimensions in sustainable way.

In the era of globalization where world has become a factory of commodification and collusion for self interest, there saving cultural heritage has becomes crucial and alarming factor in some countries. Speedy globalization has awakened the people to safeguard their legacy. People have fear to loose their cultural values and heritage due to migrants and diasporas.

Culture has potential to connect the people with environment by increasing mutual understanding and benefits. Most of the culture have originated through nature based elements. Henceforth cultural practices have been the integral part of natural phenomena. It has been observed that authenticity of culture and its various products such as costumes, food, dance, music, fairs, festivals, rituals, ceremonies, folklores, folksongs, art and craft have changed during the last few decades due to self directed knowledge transfers and impact of globalization. Nowadays its almost difficult to verify the authenticity of culture and its products or even legacy. There is a drastic change in people's attitude towards their own culture or other's culture. It may be due to more cross cultural communication and advanced technology which has given a varied dimensions to think hundred times before you talk about your culture or other's cultural heritage. Because of technology and tourism people have become more experienced and informative in regard to various types of cultures, similarities and drawbacks.

The process of eco-cultural tourism brings happiness and prosperity among both tourist and host through interactive session of learning and conservation. Eco-cultural tourism has potential to highlight the forgotten culture and solution to save it. Cultural tourists are those segments of tourists who believes in cultural conservation and heritage management. Lost glory of authentic culture can be retrieved and retained through the indigenous knowledge transfer and sharing it with responsible persons(young generation, social conservationists-cum- reformist and ecotourists).

People require resource and source of incomes or livelihood. Once income stopped or resources unavailable people adopt the path of survival of fittest which is very dangerous and led to ethnocide or genocide. And even transformed the culture, because in globalised world young people are lured to the city life by the prospect of a job, money and glamour.

Most of the cultural conflicts and clashes has been happening in the world because of people started losing faith and trust in their own culture, not because of evangelists or the people who lured the young generation showing the benefits of money, job and other options of livelihood. People are afraid due to globalisation and increasing competitions for earning money and getting food for the survival. The world has live examples where a large number of people has been killed as part of ethnocide and genocide. Some people have been trying to lure the world by power, money and status which is irrelevant and against the nature law.

One should never forgot that every culture has its own importance in the world because it originated in a certain geographical area and contains the elements which is linked with ecological system of that area. Disturbing, interfering and transforming would be completely against the rule of nature and culture too. However some awareness regarding some superstitious things can be generated among ethnic groups to save their culture in long term but not to change it completely.

"Changing culture is kind of sin against nature."

And such sin may result as disasters, calamities and uncontrollable diseases that will punish the culprits. Corona(covid-19) perhaps would be one of the best example which is originated through vanity of man.

"One culture one world" was just an assumption and it should be remained as assumption only. In real world such type of assumptions has no space because it violates the law of nature and cultural geography. Instead of spreading one culture theory evangelists must try to do something good to protect the different cultures.

Cultural tourism has contributed more than thirty percent in the overall growth of tourism sector. Eco-cultural tourism has potential to safeguard the interest of indigenous culture and its various aspects. Therefore special attention need to be given on this and any kind of hiccups should be sorted out with host communities.

Culture, Tourism And Commodification

Culture, in anthropology, the patterns of behavior and thinking that people living in social groups learn, create, and share. Culture distinguishes one human group from others. It also distinguishes humans from other animals. A people's culture includes their beliefs, rules of behavior, language, rituals, art, technology, styles of dress, ways of producing and cooking food, religion, and political and economic systems.

Cultural assets

Cultural assets or heritage is the legacy of physical artifacts and intangible attributes of a group or society that are inherited from past generations, maintained in the present and bestowed for the benefit of future generations (UNESCO). Cultural assets comprises the sources and evidence of human history and regardless of origin every community that manages to sustain or revive itself over time, there are cultural factors that contribute to the vitality and robustness of the people living there. These factors are shared and creative, which is to say they are cultural and they are assets that make life valuable, that make life worth living. These cultural assets can be material, immaterial, emotional, or even spiritual. They can be 'solid' things like concert halls, galleries, gardens, parklands and stadiums. They can be special tracts of the natural environment which encourage particular types of cultural activities. Or the climate itself might be a cultural asset if it encourages special kinds of creative and communal activities that bind people together in a place over time. Stories too might be cultural assets if they are attached to particular peoples and places if they are powerful enough to encourage people to care about and care for their place. In these stories, values can circulate, and special memories often reside in particular locations mentioned in the tales. Thus the places mentioned in the stories can be regarded as cultural assets if people tell of these places and visit them regularly and develop regular practices or rituals or ceremonies to care for them.

Heritage is a comprehensive concept that consists of many diverse values like cultural, natural, historical, architectural, archaeological, and geological values. Heritage is a mirror of different ways of lives and habits, in other words, different cultures and eras of the mankind and the society they live in. A well-preserved heritage enables communities to learn about their cultural history truly and chronologically (Pirnar I. et.al.'2012).

Cultural tourism and globalisation

Cultural tourism (or culture tourism) is the subset of tourism concerned with a country or region's culture, specifically the lifestyle of the people in those geographical areas, the history of those people, their art, architecture, religion(s), and other elements that helped shape their way of life. Cultural products are goods and services that include the arts (performing arts, visual arts, architecture), heritage conservation (museums, galleries, libraries), the cultural industries. (written media, broadcasting, film, recording), and festivals(OECD'2009).

Globalization, integration and democratization of the world's culture, economy, and infrastructure through transnational investment, rapid proliferation of communication and information technologies, and the impacts of free-market forces on local, regional and national economies. The world's globalization today leads to assimilation of individuals, peoples nations into some greater entities. The tourism industry is increasingly experiencing globalization, cultural characteristic. The stereotype of cultural globalization has Western lifestyles and forms of consumption spreading across the globe, resulting in convergence of culture. Globalization provides both positive and negative impact on cultural. Tourism is as much a political terrain as a cultural practice. It has been promoted as a route to economic development for poor nations and wielded as an instrument of political leverage between nations . As a cultural practice, tourism has been imagined as a bridge between cultures and as a form of public diplomacy, with the tourist's passport emblematic of the complex relationship between politics and culture (Molz, J.'2010).

OBJECTIVE

The objective of this research was to analyse the emerging threats due to globalisation and commodification of culture and heritage.

The specific aim was to draw attention of policy makers and planner towards culture conservation by saving authenticity and conservators.

METHODOLOGY

The paper is based on review of some literatures which indicates the nature of culture and heritage conservation. It was found that globalisation and commodification of culture has given both positive and negative impact on culture, but lost of authenticity has been emerged as a big challenge for policy makers. Eco-cultural tourism has been identified as main booster of conservation and sustainable development.

According to ICOMOS (2002), cultural heritage is an expression either tangible or intangible way of life that might developed by the community and passed down to next generation including objects, customs, practices, values, and artistic. It also define as the legacy of physical artifacts and intangible attributes that passed down from generation and for present generation to maintained and for future generation to get benefit from it (UNESCO, 2014).

Cultural sustainability was first mentioned in 1995, when the World Commission on Culture and Development (WCCD), building on the sustainable development (SD) discourse, defined cultural sustainability as inter- and intra-generational access to cultural resources (WCCD 1995). Cultural heritage is defined as ''the entire corpus of material signs - either artistic or symbolic - handed on by the past to each culture and, therefore, to the whole of humankind'' (UNESCO 1989). Tangible parts include monuments of architectural, sculptural, painted, and archeological nature and humanmade landscapes (UNESCO 1972). While intangible cultural heritage include ''practices, representations, expressions, knowledge, skills – as well as the instruments, objects, artefacts and cultural spaces associated therewith – that communities, groups and, in some cases, individuals recognize as part of their cultural heritage.'' (UNESCO 2003). In 2001 a process with the aim to add culture as the fourth sustainability dimension started with the UNESCO Universal Declaration on cultural diversity (UNESCO 2001),

Attracting and serving visitors in accordance with their needs is considered a success factor also in cultural tourism (Hausmann, 2007; duCros & Mc Kercher, 2015). Cultural tourism includes movements of persons to cultural heritage attractions with the intention to gather new information and experiences to satisfy cultural needs (WTO, 1985; Richards, 1996; Whyte et al., 2012). According to Koermo P.(2003), the cultural heritage is the process that able its significance to be presented not only for today generation, it also offer for future generation. Social and cultural sustainability dimensions lag behind economic, but also the ecological, dimension. In addition, the inclusion of social and cultural values in natural resource management and planning requires both improved knowledge and a collaborative learning process among stakeholders (Bouwen and Taillieu 2004;). Cultural heritage tourism is "traveling to experience the places and activities that authentically represent the stories and people of the past and present" [Dogsner, S. 2012]. It is an economic development tool designed to attract visitors to an area based on the unique aspects of the locality's history, landscape and culture. This not only boosts regional and local pride but is also a good source of revenue for a community and creates jobs.

Authenticity- finding genuineness of any culture that whether it is original or transformed. Defining cultural authenticity is difficult, and many authors and educators discuss the complexity of cultural authenticity rather than define it. Rudine Sims Bishop (2003) states that cultural authenticity cannot be defined but "you know it when you see it" as an insider reading a book about your own culture. No culture sees itself as having one among many possible versions of "reality." Cultural systems create genuine, authentic worlds that are experienced as "real." If this "reality" comes to be questioned seriously, it is a certainty that the culture is on the way to major transformation or collapse. In some cases the original meaning of the ritual or performance to local people is lost as the 'tourist' version takes hold (Francis, 2001). When this change continues it threatens culturally important places and artifacts. This leads to erosion of traditions where it may be seen as staged authenticity and assimilation.

Perpetuates negative stereotypes leading to ethnocentrism, may led to conflict due to cultural differences. Culture can be presented as an economic sector, and in different ways. As Organisation for Economic Cooperation and Development (OECD)' (2005:139) states, "Culture is the basis of the new economy, and is giving rise to many creative activities that produce high value-added." Cultural diversity can be considered as one of a fertile ground for cultural tourism, and it can also generate income and contribute to national economy through what is called "creative industries". Many tourists seek rural destinations which offer pleasant experiences related to the natural environment, historic heritage, and cultural patterns (Butler and Hall 1998; World Tourism Organization 1994). According to Desalegn A.(2018), rural cultural practices are heavily being influenced by globalization. For example, there is a rapid erosion of values in festivals and rituals. A simple example is traditional drinks being replaced by beer. Entering into villages, a tourist does not obviously want to experience drinking beer, but something local. The same is true with urban centers. Urbanization in Ethiopia is expanding, but major cultural flavors being dropped. In Addis Ababa, for example, there is an extensive urban renewal program. However, the old cultural systems, historic buildings, old neighborhoods are being swiped away, only to make a monotonous agglomeration of buildings with no any "Ethiopian" flavor. A tourist, who travels in Addis Ababa from one end to another, would find nothing different not only within the city itself and the city compared to other cities in the west, this assertion becoming truer and truer in the future, as current trend show.

Cultural heritage gives much more benefits towards society. It helps current generation to learn the success and mistakes that earlier generation did as a guide or make it better. It creates awareness and this makes the society to have a concrete identity, self-respect, and building up a strong country. Without cultural heritage, a society or country will lose it main source of self-expression and in the end their self-realization. From the past we learn, for the future we built(Sabrina, I.2016). The Rio conference in 1992 introduced social sustainability as the right to live a decent life; inter-generational, intragenerational, and international social justice; and local participation in SD processes. There is a strong consensus of the national population that cultural properties should be passed on to succeeding generations, and that they cannot be preserved solely by the efforts of owners and local residents. Most Japanese people are willing to pay a significant amount for heritage protection

(Kakiuchi, 2005, 2011, 2012; Kodama el al., 2007) At the same time, one of the most important values of cultural properties might be the bequest value: the value derived by people today from the expected enjoyment of heritage by future generations (ibid). It can be said that cultural properties are public goods for society as a whole, which warrants government support (Kakiuchi, 2008). According to Prentice , culture is a complex of distinct spiritual, emotional, intellectual and material features that form character to a particular society or group and its inflict on their way of life. It encapsulate a nation's soul and spirit as usually in forms of the arts, literatures, lifestyle, creativity, knowledge system, traditions, beliefs, historic buildings, sites, and other invaluable assets. It often shared, learned, transmitted across generations, adaptive, and integrated. According to Hamid, Ahmed, indicated that heritage is a mutual between creations and products (nature and man-made) that form the environment in time and space. It's a form of reality that control by local community that they inheritance by previous generation and for us to acknowledge and participate in order to maintain its novelty. Cultural heritage tourism has a number of objectives that must be met within the context of sustainable development such as; the conservation of cultural resources, accurate interpretation of resources, authentic visitors experience, and the stimulation of the earned revenues of cultural resources. Therefore, cultural heritage tourism is not only concerned with identification, management and protection of the heritage values but it must also be involved in understanding the impact of tourism on communities and regions, achieving economic and social benefits, providing financial resources for protection, as well as marketing and promotion(Joshi, P.'2014).

Several studies indicate the importance of social and cultural values for economic development (Knack and Keefer 1997; Florida 2012), rural development (Van der Ploeg et al. 2000; Sorensen 2009), and human health (Grahn and Stigsdotter 2010). This should be of great interest for areas with a declining economy and population that has been pointed out as vulnerable (Tillva¨xtverket 2011).

Commodification- Halewood and Hannam (2001) also analyze commodification considering two perspectives. One perspective identifies commodified culture with nostalgia, which contributes to maintain cultural values and diversity. The second perspective (also endorsed by Besculides, Lee, & McCormick, 2002; Carter & Beeton, 2004; McIntosh & Prentice, 1999; Richards, 1996a), identifies commodified culture with the concept of "inauthenticity," which is also blamed for depriving culture of its original value because it refers to reproduced past performances of former traditions of a society for the benefit of tourists rather than for the fulfillment of societal needs. *Tourism* as an economic activity has been blamed for the commodification of cultures. Objects and performances that were once created for local consumption become geared towards the tourism market and consequently are said to be exploited, debased and trivialised (Cohen, 1988). Such commodification can therefore be seen to destroy the authenticity of local cultural products and relationships and lead to the 'staged' or faked experiences created specifically for external consumers (MacCannell, 1976).

The dictionary definition of commodification is to make something into an object for commercial use. In terms of tourism, commodification refers to using a place's culture and the cultural artifacts to make a large enough profit to support part of the area's economy (Fiaux).In today's tourism, commodification is prevalent everywhere one looks. Whether the tourist eats at McDonald's in China or buys souvenirs in India, they are participating in commodification. The problem with commodification is that it alters the tourists' abilities to have an authentic experience and introduces a false culture into the indigenous one. McDonald's is an American originated fast-food place and it has been globalized and introduced into the cultures of many countries. This does not allow travelers to experience the native foods because fast-food places like McDonald's are more common in tourist areas than the authentic food restaurants (Fainstein).

Another example of commodification in tourism is tourist attractions like Disney World and Disney

Land. Disney parks are tourist attractions made to make money. There is minimal historical information exposed while visiting Disney parks. The history of some of the cartoon characters is shown along with the life of Walt Disney, but the basis of the park is entertainment and profit (Fainstein). Entertainment in tourism is fine, but Disney has threatened the habitats of many animals, created huge amounts of waste, and failed to incorporate an authentic historical aspect that is needed for true tourism. In terms of cultural tourism, Disney World and Disney Land do not meet the cultural requirements because of its lack of historical content (Ivanovic).

However, the use of culture for the benefit of the tourism industry has generated other debates around a process described as commodification (or commoditization), which Medina (2003) states is "the offering of cultural products and practices for money" . "Commodification is generally taken to be the process whereby ways of life, traditions and their complex symbolism are imaged and transformed into saleable products", with tangible and intangible qualities

Commodification can be seen as a good thing, but in tourism the more authentic the experience the better it is not only for the tourist, but also for the indigenous culture.

Cultural events, products and other markers are commonly used in place promotion and serve as tourist entertainment (as in the case of Balinese dance) and souvenirs (in the instance of delftware and Pataxo´ ethnic arts). Much has been written about the role that tourism has played in adaptation of cultural forms, for example 'tourist art' (Graburn, 1976), the increasing 'heritagisation' of destinations (Hewison, 1987; Walsh, 1992) and the commodification and adaptation of rituals, dances and festivals for tourist consumption (Greenwood, 1989).

RESULT AND DISCUSSION

People plan various things for the sake of fruitful results and gaining prominence in modern society. And in order to do so sometimes they come across with unlawful act or unruly behaviour which they try to avoid or ignore due to limitations of time and unlimited tasks and wants. Such ignorance might be dangerous in future prospects as it provides opportunities to flourish antisocial elements who commit crimes. In long term such crimes may become irresistible and reciprocal in terms of its dimensions and impact. So better to restrict the antisocial elements at root level itself so that it could not spread and devastate the beauty of cultures. A proper cultural planning may help in this regard to generate the cultural peace and harmony unanimously.

Cultural planning not only brings unity but also peace, harmony and prosperity among all different cultures as it provides equal rights and importance to every culture in a geographical area. It also stagnates the tendency and intention of cultural shifts.

Every culture has its own personality which consist of history, art and craft, style of architecture, ethnic food and way of preparing it, music and dance, story, mythology, fables, folklore, costumes, God and Goddess, epics, scriptures, ritual, traditions, ceremonies, processions, festivals etc. All these elements if conserved in long term and inherited from one generation to another in authentic way then it could become heritage.

Globalization has provided an opportunity to transport culture from its origin place to other parts of the world. People are migrating with their culture from one part to other parts of world for the sake of job, conferences, functions, events and business opportunities and in order to achieve their goals and settled down to host country they spread their cultural essence among local communities which gives impact in both positive and negative ways. In today's world what you see? What you observe? What you eat? What you wear? And even the way you behave might be influenced with one culture or more than one culture to some extent.

According to Modi, N.(2018) *"If we can overcome our internal problems, this interconnected world that we have if we can transform that into opportunities in the service of humanities for peace and for harmony then we together can make a huge contribution. In human history, India and China have dominated global trade for centuries. At the same time, there was no conflict. We must think of furthering connectivity without any conflict."*

Cultural heritage brings solutions to disadvantages of mass tourism, though it has of course its' own problems. The disadvantages associated with the application of cultural heritage tourism in undeveloped regions are quite a few.

Cultural Violence

The word "Man" itself is wild and violent in nature. It generates feeling of proud, arrogance, self-esteem, superiority complex, differentiation, inequalities and all other types of unruly, and unacceptable behaviour until it changed into the word "Human" (Humanity).

The word "Man" is the main reason behind conflicts and violence happening in most part of the world.

Man need to change or transform into human. Things would be ok..

Man ➡ Change ➡ Human = Peace + Prosperity (No Global Warming, No Climate Change) = Gross Happiness

Trends in Culture Conservation

Many country and academic institutions have been focused on indigenous knowledge transfer because of cultural threats, declining value of culture and saving indigenous knowledge. Each country has its own unique culture and traditions which is based on geography, ecology and environment of that area where it exists. And therefore it follows the scientifically proven things in natural settings. Number of countries have come forward to highlight and save their culture like New Zealand, France, Poland, China,

Indigenous culture has power to improve the human brains and drains. Most of these cultures have shown a traditional long lasting method of survival as well as celebrations. Live examples are there in the world, where in spite of advanced technology in agriculture and other area, people have been losing their lives due to unbeatable diseases that have been evolved like monsters. Average life span of living beings have come down across the globe due to climate change and global warming. More comfort lifestyle and thrust of worldly imitations perhaps the main reason behind all these sufferings.

Today human are not only enemies of nature but also of humanity too. Time has come when people should give respect to indigenous knowledge and cultural keeping aside the superstitious things from it (Kumar, C.2017). Orthodox people need to be treated as conservator and curator of culture. Only they should be guided to leave some superstitious things which they follow. The following figure defined the importance of orthodox people and their role in cultural conservation.

Fig.1. Defining Orthodox As Successor of Cultural Heritage(Legacy)

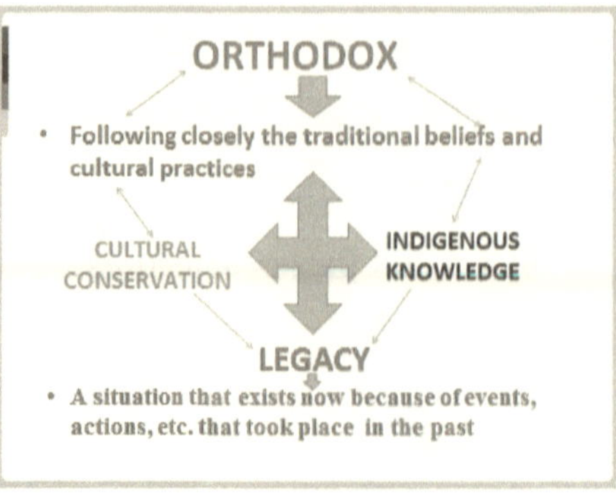

(Source: Kumar, C.'2017)

Culture and Nature

The man and woman started living together in a group to protect themselves from various natural disasters and wild animals. Living together developed a tendency to safeguard the interests of each other and natural disasters taught them lessons to adopt the life styles as per ecological systems.

Nature and its elements has been remained as integral part of culture since inception of human beings on this earth. If human beings could be able to manage this vital relationships then everything will be changed in world starting from conflicts, global warming till climate change. Interference,

Ignorance and Indulgence are the three main reasons of environmental degradation.

Q. What man will achieve leaving behind the integration and integrity?

Q. Why can't we work together for restoration of lost glory?

Q. Are we waiting for Messiah?

Q. Don't we think nature is Messiah?

Number of questions comes in mind because of shifting pattern of cultural values from positive to negative. Globalization has given the varied impact on cultural heritage in different countries but at the same time has tried to restore and conserve it. Various organisations at national and international level have been working for the sovereignty and dignity of cultural heritages including of UNESCO, ICOMOS and IUCN are some of them. But it needs to be done at individual levels to make it more effective and impactful. And cultural tourism could contribute more in conservation and sustainable development.

The following points should be kept in mind while dealing with eco-cultural tours,

I)   Briefing and de-briefing regarding itinerary to cultural sites and norms.

II)   Coordination with head of cultural village or organisers regarding sensitive issues.

III) Limitations of indigenous knowledge transfer.

IV)   Participation and restrictions to participate in festivals, fairs, rituals, and ceremonies.

V)   Learning experience through indigenous cultural activities only.

VI)   Sharing is caring, but knowing the limitations.

VII) Focus on conservation and deterioration of cultural values, if not superstitious.

VIII) Appreciating and Motivating for nature connection and conservation.

IX)   Extending help in support of their faith and trust in indigenous culture.

X)   Friendliness, honour and respect to all individuals of Community for keeping their long tradition authentic and intact.

CONCLUSION

Culture and heritage is one of the major purpose of tourism phenomenon which constitute more than thirty percent of tourism activities in the world. Responsible tourism activities would help in cultural conservation over mass tourism activities. A proper planning and promotion would led the rigid foundation of cultural conservation and sustainable development of tourism. Community and their priority should not be ignored just to satisfy the demand of tourists. And tourist should also behave in more responsible ways than earlier to protect themselves and culture of host Community. Tour operators and tour guides will have to play vital role in carrying forward the social responsibility of cultural and heritage conservation.

Cultural heritage tourism has gained a substantial attention in the tourism industry (McCain and Ray,

2003: 713-717). Because travelers are becoming more and more interested in opportunities to learn about places through their art and history, cultural tourism consistently grows. achieving the right balance between encouraging the expansion of cultural heritage tourism and protecting heritage sites, resources and monuments by educating local people and keeping the volume of tourists to heritage travel destination areas to within optimum sustainable limits (Parker, 2007). Also, within the measures to be taken to overcome the problems with the development are: Zoning, Regional planning, Licensing regulations, Control in central areas and Decentralization of cultural supply (Paulo, 2002: 165-182). When developmental and promotional strategies are analyzed; improvement in educational and cultural context of tourism, concentration of activities around important themes, strategic usage of mass media and development of out-of-season tourism seem to be the global issues concerning all areas using cultural heritage tourism for regional development.

Authenticity is just as central to the demand aspect of the cultural tourism continuum as it is to the supply aspect. On demand side, authenticity is seen as an experience. A cultural heritage attraction not purposely built for tourism use is believe to be one of a kind, irreplaceable and therefore unique. The uniqueness of a cultural attraction is a guarantee of there being no other the same, having the same significance, or revealing the same characteristics anywhere else in the world. These attractions are considered the property of the whole of humanity and can be declared World Heritage Sites by UNESCO. On inscription, the preservation of the site for future generations becomes an obligation of world community. If, for whatever reason, a country fails to maintain the high standard required for managing a world heritage site in danger list- for example, Robben Island was almost listed as such. Examples of World Heritage Sites are, Kyoto City (Japan).

The support of tourism stakeholders is essential for the development, successful operation, and long-term sustainability of tourism. Tourism stakeholders include many different types of groups depending on geographically based in the different parts of the area. However, not all stakeholders have the same level of interest in sustainable tourism development and may be less active or not active at all. Moreover, some stakeholders are more important than others in determining the success of activities. According to Freeman (1984, p.46), a stakeholder is 'any group or individual who can affect or is affected by the achievement of the organisation's objectives'. The UNWTO identified stakeholders in tourism destinations as tourism professionals, public authorities, as well as the press and other media. In addition, other interest groups and individuals and in particular local residents and indigenous groups, also need proper recognition as stakeholders in their own right (Macbeth, Burns, Chandler, Revitt, & Veitch, 2002) effective stakeholder engagement must therefore 'reduces potential conflicts between the tourists and host community by involving the latter in shaping the way in which tourism develops'.

It is confirmed that now tourists would take lessons through covid-19 like pandemic and will plan their future tourism destinations or activities on the basis of physical distancing and also distance of tourism products from crowd (human populations), air and sound pollution. The people would develop more faith in indigenous lifestyle and idea of staying in tranquility rather than disturbances which would further led the foundation of nature based tourism and Tribal (ethnic) / indigenous Tourism. People relations with nature will come more closure and distance from big malls and other manmade attractions will increase. Tourist and host both need to behave in responsible manner then earlier, that is before corona(covid-19) pandemic and will have to develop trust in each other to achieve the socio-economic goal of cultural heritage conservation through responsible tourism.

RECOMMENDATIONS

The paper came out with following recommendation to safeguard the culture and heritage of a destination from globalisation and liberalisation.

(i)   Culture should be treated as part of economic development of any nation.

(ii) Breeding local cultural ethics among the professionals, traders and service providers.

(iii)   Visit to cultural museum of the area for all types of new visitors, guests and tourists as well as businessman.

(iv)   All service providers located at the entry and exit point of city or nearby should compulsorily provide service in local cultural style irrespective of type of services or nation belongs to.

(v)   Promoting responsible and eco-cultural tourism in the area to generate learning experience and appreciations for cultural conservations.

(vi)   Developing Community Based Indigenous Knowledge Transfer System (CBIKTS) to inherit the elements of cultural conservation.

(vii)   Indigenous and orthodox people should be guided and motivated to propagate culture and heritage leaving aside superstitious elements.

(viii)   Establishing proper institution to lookafter the progress of government initiatives to safeguard the local culture and heritage from the threats of globalisation.

(ix)   Nature, culture and wildlife should be promoted together in line of carrying capacity of destination in sustainable way.

LIMITATIONS

Any generalized idea is not right due to variations in size, goal, changing perceptions, literatures reviewed and region followed.

DIRECTION FOR FURTHER RESEARCH

The further research must direct itself for conducting such investigations. This will make the applications more meaningful to make present review and opinion more effective. Further the views suggested are macroscopic; this can be further extended to microscopic level.

ACKNOWLEDGEMENT

The President., Vice President Academic, Dean- College of Agri/N/ Resources., Dean- FBE,-

Wildlife & Ecotourism, Gambella University, Gambella, Ethiopia

REFERENCES

Ahmad AG, 2006, Cultural heritage of south-east Asia: Preservation for world recognition. Journal of Malaysian Town Plan, 3: 52-62.

Bouwen, R., and T. Taillieu., 2004, Multi-party collaboration as social learning for interdependence: Developing relational knowing for sustainable natural resource management. Journal of Community & Applied Social Psychology. Special Issue: Multi-party Collaboration as Learning for Interdependence in Natural Resource Management, 14: 137–153.

Butler, R. and M. Hall, 1998, Conclusion: The Sustainability of Tourism and Recreation in Rural Areas. In Tourism and Recreation in

Rural Areas, R. Butler, M. Hall and J. Jenkins, eds., Toronto: Wiley, pp. 249–258.

Carter, R., & Beeton, R.. 2004, A model of cultural change and tourism. Asia Pacific Journal of Tourism Research, ,9(4), 423–442

Carter, R.W., 2000, Cultural change and tourism: Towards a prognostic model. PhD thesis, University of Queensland,.

Kumar, C., 2017, Ethiopian Orthodox Christianity And Jain Philosophy: A Common Interlinkage Perspective Of Cultural Conservation And Peace Building In The World, International Conference on "African and Jain Philosophies: Indigenous Enlightenment in Peace Building", Mekelle University, Ethiopia on 17 and 18 May.

Cohen, E. 2001, Ethnic tourism in Southeast Asia. In T. Chee-Beng, S.C.H. Cheung and H. Yang (eds) Tourism, Anthropology and China, Singapore: White Lotus Press., pp. 27-53.

Fisher, J., 1993, Thr road from Rio: Sustainable development and the non-governmental movement in the Third World. Westport, CT: Praeger,.

Florida, R., 2012, The rise of the creative class, revisited. New York: Basic Books.

Freeman, R. E., & Gilbert, D. R., 1987, Managing stakeholder relationships. In S. P. Sethi & C. M. Falbe (Eds.), Business and society: Dimensions of conflict and cooperation Lexington: Lexington Books, pp. 397-423.

Freeman, R. E. 1984, Strategic management: A stakeholder approach. Boston: Pitman.

Frykman, J,2002, Place for something else. Analysing a cultural imaginary. Ethnologia Europaea _/ Journal of European Ethnology, 32 (2), 47-68.

Grahn, P., and U.K. Stigsdotter, 2010, The relation between perceived sensory dimensions of urban green space and stress restoration. Landscape and Urban Planning, 94: 264–275.

Hausmann, A., 2007, Cultural Tourism: Marketing Challenges and Opportunities for German Cultural Heritage. International Journal of Heritage Studies, Vol. 13, Iss. 2, 171–185.

https://tourismandculture.weebly.com/commodi fication.html/retrieved/2015

https://www.academia.edu/34565640/preserving _cultural_heritage_and_possible_impacts_on_re gional_development_case_of_izmir_research_as sist._kamil_yağci

https://www.worldpoliticsreview.com/articles/7 144/tourism-global-culture-and-transnational-diplomacy/retrieved 2015

Kakiuchi, E., (Ed.), 2011, Evaluating the heritage values (in Japanese). Tokyo, Japan: Suiyo-sha.

Kakiuchi, E., 2012, Sustainable cities with creativity: Promoting creative urban initiatives: Theory and practice in Japan. In L. F. Girard, T. Baycan, & P. Nijkamp (Eds.), Sustainable city and creativity: Promoting creative urban initiatives, UK: Ashgate Publishing Limited, 413-440..

Kakiuchi, E., 2008, The possible model for culture-based tourism development in Japan: Implication of CVM survey of the World Heritage of Gokayama, Toyama Prefecture, Japan. In UNWTO, Tourism and community development: Asian practice, Madrid, Spain: UNWTO, pp. 163-183.

Knack, S., and P. Keefer, 1997, Does social capital have an economic payoff? A cross-country investigation. Quarterly Journal of Economics,112: 1251–1288.

Kodama, Y., Tamazawa et al.,2007, An economic analysis of cultural capital's value: A study of Miyajiama, Hiroshima (in Japanese). Journal of the City Planning Institute of Japan, 42(1), 93-99.

Koermo P., 2003, Heritage in Malaysia: The national conservation programs for national heritage in Malaysia. In the 2nd IFSAH 2003 & International Symposium on Asian Heritage by

Urban Design and Conservation Research Unit (UDCRU), Faculty of Built Environment, Universiti Teknologi, Malaysia.

Kumar, C. and Choudhary, A, 2016, Ecotourism Planning Development & Marketing, Bharti Publications, New Delhi, India.

Macbeth, J., Burns et al., 2002, Community as tourism object: associated disciplinary understandings. Paper presented at the CAUTHE conference.

MacIntosh, R. and Goeldner, C., 1990, Tourism Principles, Practices and Philosophies (6th edn). New York: John Wiley and Sons.

Narendra Modi, 2018, Participating in a dialogue titled 'Transforming Asia through Innovation', Nanyang Technological University, Singapore.

National Trust for Historic Preservation, Heritage Tourism, http://www.preservationnation.org/information-center/economics-ofrevitalization/heritage-tourism/#.UTO_fTk_644/S. Doganer-2012/

OECD-1.2005, Culture and Local Development.

Organisation for Economic Cooperation and Development,2009, The Impact of Culture on Tourism. OECD, Paris.

P.V. Joshi, 2012, Planning Cultural-Heritage Tourism for Sustainable Development. Golden Research Thoughts, 1 XI.

Parkes, S., 1997, Understanding Contemporary Germany. London: Routledge.

Reid, D., 2000, Cultural tourism: Learning from the past. In J. Akama and P. Sterry (eds) Cultural Tourism in Africa: Strategies for the New Millennium. Proceedings of the ATLAS Africa International Conference.

Reid, D. et.al.,1999, Tourism, bio-diversity and community development. In D. Reid (ed.) Ecotourism Development in Eastern and Southern Africa. Harare: Weaver Press.

Richards, G. (ed.), 2001, Cultural Attractions and European Tourism. Wallingford: CABI.

Richards, G. (ed.),1996, Cultural Tourism in Europe. Wallingford: CABI.

Richards, G., 1996, The Scope and Significance for Cultural Tourism. In: G. Richards (Ed.), Cultural Tourism in Europe, Wallingford: CABI, pp. 21-39.

Sabrina I., 2016 Understanding the Significance of Cultural Attribution, Anthropology, Malaysia.

Sorensen, T., 2009, Creativity in rural development: An Australian response to Florida. International Journal of Foresight and Innovation Policy, 5: 24–43.

Stephen Wearing & John Neil, 2009, Ecotourism: Impacts, Potentials and Possibilities, Butterworth-Heinemann, UK.

UNESCO, 2002, World Heritage Papers, no. 7. Paris.

UNESCO, 2010, The power of culture for development. Paris.

UNESCO, 2001,Universal declaration on cultural diversity. Records of the general conference, 31st session, Paris, France. Resolutions. Paris, Annex I, Volume 1.

UNESCO, 2003, Cultural landscapes: The challenges of conservation. Proceedings of the workshop, Ferrara, Italy.

UNESCO.1972, Convention concerning the protection of the world cultural and natural heritage. Adopted by the General Conference at its seventeenth session, Paris, France. Paris.

Uslaner, E., 1999, Democracy and social capital. In Democracy and trust, ed. M.E. Warren, 121–150. Cambridge: Cambridge University Press.

Van der Duim, V.R., 2003, 'Tourismscapes'. An Essay on Tourism, Globalization and Sustainability. To be presented to the Research Conference 'Managing on the Edge: Shifts in the Relationship between Responsibility, Governance and Sustainability', University of Nijmegen.

Van der Ploeg, J.D, et al. 2000, Rural development: From practices and policies towards theory. Sociologia Rural 40: 391–408.

Verburg, D., 2004, Cultural tourism as an arena: A case study from Tanzania. MSc thesis, Wageningen University, Wageningen.

Wallerstein, I., 2000, 'Cultures in conflict? Who are we? Who are the others?', Y.K. Pao Distinguished Chair Lecture, Center for Cultural Studies, Hong Kong University of Science and Technology.

WCCD, 1995, Our creative diversity, 64 pp. Paris.

WCED.1987, Our common future. Report of the World Commission on Environment and Development, 247 pp. New York: United Nations.

Whyte, B., Hood, T. and White, B., 2012, Cultural and Heritage Tourism: A Handbook for Community Champions, Ottawa: Federal Provincial Territorial Ministers of Culture and Heritage.

Wiranatha, A.S., 2001, A systems model for regional planning towards sustainable development in Bali, Indonesia. PhD thesis, University of Queensland.

World Tourism Organization (WTO) ,1985, The Role of Recreation Management in the Development of Active Holidays and Special Interest Tourism and the Consequent Enrichment of the Holiday Experience. Madrid: World Tourism Organization.

WTO, 1994. National and Regional Tourism Planning: Methodologies and Case Studies.

WTTC Report , 2015, Travel and Tourism Economic Impact.

---@@---

(page purposely kept blank)

CHAPTER 5

Scapegoat Marketing: An International Business Opportunity through Covid-19 Concept

The globalisation has produced many challenges on the face of the world and the outbreak in diseases like Covid-19 treated as one of the dangerous challenge that the whole world has been facing since for the past several months. When business dealings not ended with some common solutions then got transformed into SAR, or Covid-19 like viruses on time to time basis. Global warming, climate change and other environmental degradation are the result of human encroachment towards the nature. But who bothers about it? Neither consumers nor producers of products. People have become opportunist rather than optimist. Everyone is looking for an excuse and an opportunity to ruin the other for dominancy.

It is well said " No Gain, Without Pain". And to ground the gain now countries started taking and giving pain in the form of Covid-19 (scapegoat business marketing).

The scapegoat business marketing aimed at unfortunate trade war between countries to become a global business leader by sacrificing their own people and transforming people of other countries into a scapegoat or parasite who could not survive without others help. The present scenario of business has undergone with a drastic change where red ocean strategy is dominant over blue ocean due to real "cutting- throat" competition.

The value of human life and humanity have nothing to do before Money, Wealth and Power(MWP). The only thing that matters is "Wealth and Power," and to achieve this, the failed warriors can go to any extent, even to devastations. Let's understand the MWP in the context of Covid-19(Corona Virus),

> I)   *Money* : which is brighter than sunshine sweeter than honey has

power to buy many. Hence, *Money = Many*.

II)   *Wealth:* Now the concept of health has been changed into " *Wealth is Health*" means countries and their people's health would totally depend on their wealth.

III)   *Power:* it's kind of addiction which has become more dangerous than narcotic drugs such as Cocaine and Heroin. If no one is ready to nail-down, prestige hurts; then apply Scapegoat Business Marketing.

Covid-19 : popularly know as Novel Corona Virus'2019 has increased the morbidity rate and homelessness in many countries is basically a concept virus to stabilize the 'trembling economy of country by tumbling bay'.

Scapegoat Business Marketing has become very common strategy in order to overcome with the problems of economy slowdown, wealth crisis and superiority complex. The main concept of such strategy is to paralyze the economy of other countries by sacrificing some people. This way pressure would not only decrease on the scarce resources of the country but also on accumulated wealth, which would propagate the power through recovery (business opportunities) in other countries in short term and business in long term.

The present scenario could be seen as one of the best example where concept country would dominant over other by transforming them into parasite due to sudden outbreak in disease(Covid-19). The business opportunities would be in producing health equipments and accessories which is life saving essential needs. Through time bound and fast recovery, such concept country would try to develop trust in market regarding their health system and products. The severely affected countries naturally got attracted towards concept country and placed business orders. The concept country offers long term loan-support to the poor countries to establish everlasting business relationship without much analysis. The underdeveloped countries becomes parasite for concept country and some developed countries treated as scapegoat.

The concept country also develop political framework of support with some specified countries to sell their health products. Such parasite or scapegoat countries becomes ambassador for concept country for time being until business rapport got well established. Concept country should never forget that the business opportunity which is built on heinous crimes could not be able to stay in long run due to leakage and partial loyalty.

Such outbreak in viral disease also provides opportunities to the countries good in information technology and software development due to the lock down and practices of social distancing to avoid infection. But again software is of no use without computer hardware so provides opportunities to countries good in computer hardware development. In such pandemic situation if any country thinks that they could run their business in isolation then it would be a kind of fooling yourself. People easily gets afraid with death and to save their lives they can go the any extent. Here Scapegoat Business Marketing works.

Scapegoat Marketing will have very dangerous impact on the world economy, environment and natural ecosystem. Underdeveloped and poor countries will have to suffer a lot due to cold war and wealth war like situations. It would produce new type of slavery in the world.

A Report on Corona (Covid-19) and Political Scenario

Despite calls for global cooperation, US and China spar over leading COVID response. The U.S. and Chinese governments have increasingly turned the novel coronavirus pandemic into a contest over their primacy as the world's leading humanitarian force. The U.S. and Chinese governments have increasingly turned the novel coronavirus pandemic into a contest over their primacy as the world's leading humanitarian force, with Secretary of State Mike Pompeo highlighting U.S. contributions to global aid agencies Tuesday and pushing back on Chinese propaganda about its overseas assistance.

But as the pandemic spreads to the developing world and kills more people in nearly every region, experts say a lack of global coordination has cost the world time, money, and lives, with some saying U.S. leadership has been missing.

"This pandemic can only be won when countries and means and resources are put and pooled together to contain and to fight the spread of the virus," Robert Mardini, director-general designate of the International Committee of the Red Cross, told ABC News. "This is the only way forward."

 U.S. contributions to global agencies far surpass China's -- $400 million to the World Health Organization, compared to China's $44 million; $700 million to UNICEF, compared to China's $16 million; and $1.7 billion to the United Nations High Commissioner for Refugees (UNHCR), compared to $1.9 million from China.

Senior U.S. officials have also accused the Chinese government of attaching "strings" to their assistance.

"The Chinese Communist Party has a special responsibility to provide no-strings-attached assistance around the world and take responsibility for what everyone realizes is the result of the cover-up that happened in Wuhan," James

Richardson, director of the State Department's office of foreign assistance resources, said Thursday, although he did not provide evidence of China attaching any conditions to its aid.

Instead, some countries have welcomed Chinese assistance and praised Beijing for providing much-needed medical supplies or sharing data and know-how. Ethiopia's health minister thanked Chinese officials for "sharing valuable experience" and helping "improve the capacity of Africa in containing COVID-19," while the African Union's commissioner of social affairs praised Chinese "cooperation ... to fight COVID-19 in the continent," including the supply of more than 10,000 lab testing kits.

But other countries have pushed back on Beijing, reporting that Chinese-provided tests or other medical supplies have been defective. The Dutch Health Ministry said over the weekend that 600,000 medical masks from China would not be used and some would be recalled after distribution because they did not fit or work properly. In Spain, health authorities said tens of thousands of tests, out of hundreds of thousands from China, were defective, with Turkey and the Czech Republic reporting similar issues.

The European Union's top diplomat, Josep Borrell, warned that the U.S. and China are competing in "a struggle for influence through spinning and the 'politics of generosity.'"

"China is aggressively pushing the message that, unlike the U.S., it is a responsible and reliable partner. In the battle of narratives, we have also seen attempts to discredit the EU as such, and some instances where Europeans have been stigmatized as if all were carriers of the virus," Borrell said, an apparent reference to Trump's restriction on travel from Europe that he initially cast as a Europe-wide ban and that was issued without European consultation, a senior European diplomat told ABC News at the time.

Pompeo's statement also seemed intended to quell a domestic audience. With testing insufficient to broadly trace and isolate cases in the U.S., and shortages of equipment like face masks and ventilators putting the lives of medical professionals and patients at risk, there has been anger over U.S. assistance to other countries.

In particular, the State Department helped send 17.8 tons of personal protective equipment, or PPE, and other medical supplies from U.S. charities, including Samaritan's Purse and the Mormon Church, to Wuhan in early February. Pompeo tweeted video of their arrival in China, saying they "can help save lives in #China and help protect people from the #coronavirus."

"Trump, you incompetent idiot! You sent 18 tons of PPE to China early but ignored warnings & called COVID19 concerns a hoax. You've endangered doctors, nurses, aids, orderlies, & janitors - all risking their lives to save ours," tweeted Rep. Maxine Waters, D-Calif., chair of the House Financial Services Committee -- although those supplies didn't come from the nation's stockpiles.

The U.S. has offered $274 million to assist 64 different countries and UNHCR in combatting the pandemic, and Pompeo said Tuesday those funds are key to keeping the American people safe as well.

"In America, we provide aid because we're a generous and noble people. We also do it because we know from prior experiences that [if] we don't have good data, full transparency, and all-out effort to fight pandemics, that can harm Americans back home, too," he said.

But experts have called for a global effort to combat the pandemic, arguing that individual countries alone, battling over medical resources or finger-pointing about the virus' origins, will not solve this crisis. The U.S., however, has made no public effort to bring together like-minded countries, and foreign ministers from the G7 alliance of democracies failed to issue a joint statement on the pandemic after Pompeo insisted the group call it the "Wuhan virus."

"Unfortunately, even as COVID-19 accelerates inside our country, the Trump administration seems to view diplomacy as a bludgeon to score points against adversaries and alienate friends rather than an essential tool for helping to protect Americans," tweeted Brett McGurk, a senior diplomat under George W. Bush and Barack Obama who served as special envoy to the Global Coalition to Defeat ISIS until he resigned over Trump's ordered withdrawal from Syria.

The presidents of Germany, Singapore, Ethiopia, and Ecuador, and the king of

Jordan authored a joint op-ed in the Financial Times on Tuesday, calling for a new global alliance to convene the "medical, economic, and political elements required to produce a vaccine for all who need it" and ensure that testing kits are produced quickly and distributed widely and fairly.

"This is a global crisis. Delay in action means death. We all face the same enemy and we stand to gain by bringing the full force of humanity together to fight it," the five leaders wrote. "Before this virus, we are all equal and must work together to beat it."

Source: ABC News's Mel Madarang contributed to this report'2020).

(Page purposely kept blank)

CHAPTER 6

CORONA(Covid-19) AND TOURISM: MORE OPPORTUNITIES IN THE AFTERMATH OF THE LOCKDOWN

Abstract

The Corona(covid-19) crisis and conditional lockdown by several countries have generated tendency of " *escape for change*" among locked people. Lockdown can be seen as an opportunity to see more tourists and tourism in coming days. The paper is based on opinion of author, review of some literature and discussion with scholars, professors and other key stakeholders in tourism. The paper found Corona(covid-19) and lockdown as an opportunity to improve and explore new horizon of tourism with more improved infrastructure and service.

Key words: corona, covid-19, global trade, hospitality, innovation, lockdown, tourism, wildlife

1. Introduction

In recent times, Covid-19 (Coronavirus) can be seen as precursor of natural balancing act of the nature. Coronavirus is a form of the infinite culmination of man, which is born due to human mistakes. Man has repeatedly ignored nature and in order to fulfill his infinite aspirations, he has exploited the flora and fauna day and night.

Tourism has also not been untouched by this calamitous disaster like coronavirus. This sudden disaster has also created challenges in front of a beautiful, peaceful, nurturing and eco-friendly business like tourism. But due to many challenges, creative and influential services are being built. All these services can be divided into *health, safety and eco friendly services.*

2. Major Impact of Lockdown

Many countries have imposed lockdown to control the intensity of transmission of Corona virus (covid-19). People of these countries are bounded to follow the imposed rules and regulations to protect their family members from disaster. But such situations generate more agitated kind of environment due to more comfort zone. And people start feeling as if somebody has kept them in a cage. Henceforth, psychologically these locked people generate *"flying attitude"* like any bird who is looking for chance to escape. Tourism is the best way to escape to satisfy the psychic gratification. People would always look for change and that change need to be tapped by the tour operators, travel agents, hoteliers, destination management and marketing organisations. The demand of tourism will increase, but mostly for nature based, adventure, leisure, rural and spiritual odyssey tourism. The counties have "wet market" like China, Vietnam, some African and South American countries will have to suffer initially but again scenario will change over the period of time. Tourist have lost trust in host communities in many countries and similarly host countries have also lost trust in tourists that need to be rebuilt. But, it will take a some time to regain it.

2.1. Positive Impact

i) Increased rate of tourist flow at tourism destinations due to lockdown.

ii) Emerging of new tourism destinations and change in destination image.

iii) Sudden increase in family outings to nearby nature based tourism spot.

iv) Rise of Neighbour Tourism, rural tourism, Agri-tourism and city Tourism.

v) Improved standard in health, travel, communication, shopping and hygiene-sanitations.

vi) Promotion of eco-friendly products and change in food habit of tourists and guests.

vii) Tourism advocacy – more awareness regarding nature, culture and ecology.

viii) Restrictions on wildlife trade/ wet market.

ix)   Accelerate sense of conservation of biodiversity.

x)   Boost in domestic tourism.

2.2. Negative Impact

i)   Decreased buying capacity of tourists

ii)   Tourism psychosis

iii)   Drop in long haul trip/destinations

iv)   Racism and cultural differentiations

v)   Slow visitors exports

vi)   Job loss in unorganised sector of tourism and alternative accommodation sector.

vii)   Negative BoP(Balance of Payment) due to more domestic tourism.

3. Beneficiary Tourism Destinations

The report of World Health Organisation(WHO'2020) on

Corona(Covid-19) pandemic and casualties in different countries and imposed conditional lockdown situations reveals that, the following countries and destinations, would be emerged as potential beneficiary. The global trade war and group formations on political ground also indicates the same. Revenue loss of tourism and hospitality sector never going to be compensated or recovered in future due to *perishable characteristic* of product inventories.

3.1. Indian Sub-continent

India is going to be emerged as one of the trustworthy destination both in terms of international and domestic tourism. Destination like Jammu and Kashmir, Leh & Ladakh, Orissa, North East and other destinations that have potential to pull the "lockdown mass" would emerge as main destinations for psychic gratification. City tourism, neighbour tourism, Agri-tourism, and education tourism would play a major role, atleast for two years from the date of recovery from Corona disaster. Henceforth other domestic destinations will resume with minimal impact.

3.2. African Continent

Africa will continue to receive tourist but that would totally depend on the condition and availability of open "wet market" in the African countries. Kenya, Ethiopia, Tanzania, Namibia and Egypt will keep on receiving minimal number of tourists. But other countries will have to develop more trust regarding health hazards. Again wildlife tourism and indigenous cultural tourism would be dominant in addition to geomorphological and paleoanthropological sites in these countries. Man-made attraction in Egypt will continue as main attraction.

3.3. American Continent

Caribbean Islands will continue to enjoy tourists in future. South American countries will take time to recover because of global economic crisis particularly in USA and China.

3.4. Asian Countries

Japan, Taiwan, South Korea, Mongolia, Nepal and Philippines would continue with minimal tourists receipts. Malaysia, Indonesia and Vietnam could also grab opportunity from neighbour tourism.

3.5. Australia

Australia will get more international tourists in coming years. Even New Zealand will see more number of tourists.

3.6. Russia

In European country Russia could be able to manage its minimal performance as inbound and outbound destination.

3.7. Island Countries

Island Countries like Mauritius, Fiji, Seychelles, and other will take time to recover. But it does not mean that these countries would not be able to regain it's past performance.

4. Non- Beneficiary

4.1. China

China is going to become main victim of Corona outbreak. But again in long run place like "Wuhan" would emerge as corona tourism's destination of the world.

4.2. European Destinations

The future of European tourism destinations would totally depend on global economy. Regional tourism can be promoted with domestic tourism.

4.3. North America

Northern and Western America province would face more challenging in resuming tourism activities than Eastern and southern province. Due to appreciation of other US Dollar America would be remained as tourist generating zone but will face problem in retaining inbound tourist market due global Economic crisis.

4.4. Middle East And Gulf Countries

The country could become victim of catastrophe of covid-19 due global trade war and economic crisis in the aftermath of the scapegoat business marketing.

5. Conclusion

Corona(covid-19) pandemic will have both positive and negative impact on tourism. The impact will vary from country to country. Corona crisis has brought more innovation and positive impact through various untapped opportunities. Country need to tape those opportunities through destination marketing organisation. Lockdown could be seen as big boon for the growth of tourism sector. Tourism stakeholders should grab this opportunity by monitoring, evaluating and forecasting the dormant demand which is locked inside the hoses in lockdown and waiting to escape for long term change immediately or afterwards. It would be advisable to keep eye for detail to bring dynamism in tourism through more creativity and curiosity. Tourism and Hotel industry could see more domestic tourists than international tourists in next two years. Luxury and first class segment of hotels will have to suffer with room revenue crisis due to decrease in international clients. But higher segments of hotels could survive by offering more discounted rate on their rooms, that is maintaining 60-65% RevPAR(Revenue Per Available Room) and implementing nice strategy of service mix around food. Large size travel agency and airlines will have to cut their revenue index by 30-40% instead of increasing.

Tourism will grow until human being is there on this Earth.

6. Limitations

Any generalized idea is not right due to variations in size, goal, changing perceptions and region and literatures followed.

7. Direction to further research

The further research must direct itself for conducting such investigations. This will make the study more meaningful to find linkage more effectively.

References

- Kumar Chiranjib, 03/2020, Corona(covid-19) and Tourism: Moving Forward In The Aftermath of The Fall, Academia.edu, Articles/Research note

- https://www.who.int/emergencies/diseases/novel-coronavirus-2019

- https://tourismjournals.asia/Articles-/-Insight/corona(covid-19) And Tourism/04-2020

(page purposely kept blank)

CHAPTER 7

CORONA(COVID-19) PANDEMIC AND SOLUTIONS: OPPORTUNITY THROUGH BROTHERHOOD, HOLISTIC ACTIVITIES AND UNIVERSAL ACCEPTANCE

ABSTRACT

Corona(covid-19) pandemic has again projected the glimpses of hidden agenda of differentiations, racism, vanity, inequality and self-sustainability. Love, affection, peace and harmony have been lost prior to coming to the boundaries of the nations. The paper focuses on the forgotten heroes of the united world. This world is connected and one negative energy will destroy the world, if brotherhood, holistic activities and universal acceptance are missing from actions and reactions. Time is not too far, when the earth will shrink because of misdeeds of its inhabitants. Lockdown can't be solution of global crisis. Connectedness, humanity and love for nature could be the solutions for existence.

Key word: activity, caring, brotherhood, corona(covid-19), nature, unity, universal acceptance

1. INTRODUCTION

It seems people have forgot about the theory of holistic activity, brotherhood and universal acceptance in the catastrophe of Corona(covid-19). This world is connected and it is the time when each country of this world could be remained united, irrespective of caste, creed, race, religion and trade to cope up with the corona crisis. This whole world is connected like a family and if any member of the family is not getting proper care in any part of the world, then that would be considered as failure of all. Hence lockdown can't be considered as solution of global crisis. Only collaborative approach could create win-win situations. The old verse (shloka) from Indian scripture is still applicable today in true sense.

Invention and Innovation has given so many things to people by providing comfort, but at the same time it has decreased the natural strength, immune system, and mental health of the people.

Nature and indigenous culture has power to improve the human brains and drains. Most of these cultures have shown a traditional long lasting method of survival through faith and celebrations. Live examples are there in the world, where in spite of advanced technology in agriculture and other area, people have been losing their lives due to unbeatable diseases evolved like monsters. Average life span of living beings have come down across the globe due to climate change and global warming. More comfort lifestyle and thrust of worldly imitations perhaps the main reason behind all these sufferings. Today human are not only enemies of nature but also of humanity too. Time has come when people should give respect to indigenous knowledge and cultural assets keeping aside the superstitious things from it.

1.1.   Experience Connectedness

No one is alone in this connected world. Everyone is connected to everything and the universe. Experience this connectivity which is sometime visible and sometimes not. It may seems virtual but actually it is a true world wide web (www). Any thought word, action by any one of us has an impact to the totality of universe. As for the law of transformation of energy is concerned, the sum of total of energy in the universe is constant. It can neither be created nor destroyed and it can only be transformed from one state to another. This applies to all our thoughts, all our words and actions. So we are connected to everybody and to everything in the universe. One should be careful on what they think, say or do. One should think positive, speak positive and do positive things. This experience of connectedness is Visvaroop Darshan (visualisation of God nature) or realization. This is also called *Constant Integrated Awareness (CIA)*. Experience the oneness.

"Sacrifice the Limitedness". Ahankar (ego) is the mind's identification with the limited body. Thyaga is sacrifice. True sacrifice is, sacrifice of our limitedness, so that we expand into unlimitedness (infinite). This is what the Upanishads mean when they declared "*Thyagenaike Amrutatva Manasu* – Only through sacrifice one attains immortality". Selfless Service is a good vehicle to expand to our full potential through sacrifice of ego. This is the final frontier in the journey towards self-realization. Serve All. Sacrifice what you are not (ego) and be what you really (atma) are, your true self (Atma).

The following quotation in Sanskrit from ancient Indian Scripture(Upanishads) that tell us to leave in eternal peace always..

- ॐ सर्वे भवन्तु सुखिनः (Om Sarve Bhavantu Sukhinah)
- सर्वे सन्तु निरामयाः । (Sarve Santu Nir-Aamayaah)
- सर्वे भद्राणि पश्यन्तु (Sarve Bhadraanni Pashyantu)
- मा कश्चिद्दुःखभाग्भवेत् । (Maa Kashcid-Duhkha-Bhaag-Bhavet)
- ॐ शान्तिः शान्तिः शान्तिः ॥ (Om Shaantih Shaantih Shaantih)

Meaning:

- Om(Hey God !), May All become Happy!
- May All be Free from Illness!
- May All See what is Auspicious!
- May no one Suffer!
- Om(Hey God!) Grace all with Peace, Peace and Peace !

The above quotation of ancient time is now more applicable to fight against global warming and climate change by spreading peace and harmony among people, but it would only be possible if, everyone in this world give respect and honour to each other that is living and non-living. And no doubt in this that age old indigenous culture, scriptures, epics and great philosophical thoughts of ancient philosophers are still applicable, implementable and alive and would be alive till the existence of the world through its successors.

World has witnessed many people come and go that represent this.

"Help if you can always - Even if you cannot help – Do no harm"

Purana(great epics/scriptures of India) also says(in Sanskrit Language),

"Astadasa Puranesu Vyasena Vachanam Dwayam,

Paropakaraya Punyaya – Papaya Para Peedanam"

It means essence of 18 puranas is "helping others is punya(good/blessings of God) and hurting others is papa(evil/sin)". "Make a difference with your presence". Our presence should bring in a positive change in the place or people. This should be the case in all places, in all times, in all circumstances. Attitude of gratitude help us connect and experience our blessings.

All evangelist, religious teachers, scholars, authors, philosophers and politicians should agree to work hard to bridge the gap of which is formed due to **nuisance.**

2. **CONCLUSION**

Eternal peace building among human beings can only help to fight against corona(covid19), global warming and climate change. People need to learn how to satisfy their unlimited wants with limited resources available to them in their surroundings. And in this process indigenous cultural methods and doctrines of great philosophers could contribute to maximum to human beings for getting eternal peace. Please don't forget the goal of God nature and continue with concept of holistic *activities, brotherhood and universal acceptance.* Lockdown and blaming each-other is not a solution. Solution is hidden in the treasure of eternal peace that need to be explored calmly. People need to think multiple times before manufacturing and procuring the instruments of mass destruction. Focus should be given on organic food farming. *Politicians should show their power in healing the people, rather killing the people. Save nature, save yourself and others. Everything in nature is connected therefore people have to feel it with zeal.*

3. LIMITATIONS OF EXISTING STUDY

Any generalized idea is not right due to variations in size, goal, changing perceptions and region and literatures followed.

4. SCOPE OF RESEARCH

The further research must direct itself for conducting such investigations. This will make the study more meaningful to find linkage more effectively. Further the suggested linkages need to be tested for its authenticity across the destinations and literatures available and benchmarks to be identified for others to follow. Further the views suggested are macroscopic; this can be further extended to microscopic level.

5. ACKNOWLEDGEMENT

The National President and General Secretary-Digambar Jain Mahasabha(AIDJHPO) Delhi India, President & Vice President Academic, Dean- College of Agri/N/ Resources., Dean- FBE, HoD- Wildlife & Ecotourism, Gambella University, Ethiopia

REFERENCES

- Chiranjib Kumar, 2017, Ethiopian Orthodox Christianity And Indian Jain Philosophy: A Common Interlinkage For Saving Cultural Heritage And Indigenous Knowledge In Peace Building, International Conference on African and Jain Philosophies: Indigenous Enlightenment in Peace Building, Makelle University Ethiopia..
- Diwakar S. C., Glimpse of Jainism, Published by Shri Bharatvarshiya Digambar Jain Mahasabha/04-2017
- http://www.culturalindia.net/indian-religions/mahavira.html/04-2017
- https://peepintojainism.com/jainism_vs_christianity.html/04-2017
- http://www.senamirmir.com/theme/5-2001/gh/drgh.html/04-2017
- http://www.ethiopianorthodox.org/english/calendar.html/04-2017

(Page purposely kept blank)

(Page purposely kept blank)

CHAPTER 8

MIGRATION AND CULTURE : PERSPECTIVE OF DIASPORA TOURISM

INTRODUCTION

When a person migrates, he migrates with his own culture, belief, perception, knowledge, food habits, education, experience and other backgrounds. And during interaction with host population he shares the Sam things that he poses but at the same time he/she gains the same things from host in the form of socio-cultural impact. The impact of interaction may be positive or negative on migrants and host country. Therefore preparedness of host and awareness regarding migrants in advance becomes very important to gain the benefits in long term. Migrants and Diasporas should be given opportunity to showcase their skill, talents, technology and cultures through some platform like exhibition, events or festival.

Migration of culture is good provided this is not permanent. Otherwise it would be difficult to save any culture for king time through generation to generation. Globalization has already killed the originality and authenticity of culture but at the same time it has generated a huge awareness regarding any culture throughout the world.

Diasporas are culturally hybridized (Brinkerhoff, 2003) and their transnational roots enable them to serve as a potentially important link between the two cultures, as well as to assemble considerable resources. This places Diaspora groups into a strategically important position in terms of advancing their homelands – socially, economically, and politically. They are a powerful force that can mobilize tangible foreign assistance efforts – a force that cannot be ignored by mainstream development actors. For Example,

Society and Culture:

- establishing virtual forums – mediated by ICTs – of Diaspora experts who advise home country decision makers on a variety of topics;

- creating online discussion groups, blogs, and web casts to ensure a Diaspora's own cultural integration/reintegration into home societies, as well as to facilitate participation in the decision-making process for home community development;

- using the Internet as a transnational sphere where Diasporas can produce and debate narratives of history, culture, democracy and identity. Diasporas have used the Internet to mobilize demonstrators, revamp political processes, amass funds, debate issues, rearticulate values, and ultimately influence their home governments;

- producing ethnic (Internet) radio and/or television programs that make Diasporas "present" in their home communities. Such discourse can be influential in the formation of political and economic development;

- donating free Internet connection time and text messaging to further enhance virtual communications between Diaspora groups and their home country counterparts;

In addition to more 'traditional' development efforts, the advancement of ICT is helping Diasporas to become more involved in cultural activities that benefit both themselves and their homelands. In the case of Virtual Jerusalem, for example, prayers from the Diaspora can be sent via e-mail to Jerusalem's Western Wall, which has become a pilgrimage site for Jews. Similarly, *Hindus in the Diaspora have access to a number of online puja services to show reverence to their deities. Saranam.com, for instance, is a web-based Hindu ritual service that allows believers to order a special puja in the temple of their choice.*

Diasporas, Diversities and Development (3D) are interlinked with Migration that creates challenges which further generates the new opportunities for sustainable development, creativity, innovativeness and dynamism in the prospering economy and socio-economic structure of that area where it persist. Impact might be felt positive or negative but the focuses should be on Knowledge, Technology Transfer,

International Trade and Globalization of Humanity, Harmony and Human innovation (3H). Mobility and development are the interdependent phenomenon. Therefore restrictions on mobility would stop the growth and development of each aspect of social, physical and virtual life of globalized world. Migration and diasporas has posed a big challenge for policy makers on the ways of reforms and transforming development. But one should never forget that migration creates diversities, which is important for innovation and sustainable development. Diversity helps people learn about other ways of life and what goes on in other places of the world. It brings variety to almost every part of our ways of life. Diversity helps people to better appreciate humanity and human rights in general.

Key questions are,

Q. Have we ever thought that why migration?

Ans- Not just for the livelihood but also for finding the new Approach, Appreciation and Alignment (3A).

Q. What motivates people and animals to migrate?

Ans- Change and Need

Q. What if knowledge and innovation would have not been migrated?

Ans- It would have been died a long back.

It must be understood that migration is a voluntary process most of the time but forced migration is very common in these days due to anarchy like situation in some parts of the world. And the main actor is blind globalization and one sided concentrated growth structures throughout the world. Migration should not be mixed with refugees and in same manner refugees must not be mixed with Diasporas to create controversy or conflicts. They are not even synonyms of each other. Political infiltration also can't be considered as migration.

However migration can be synonyms of "need" but not of "wants".

The present paper focuses on three dimensional things that contains three different elements such as,

1. Diasporas, Diversities and Development (3D): Diasporas brings Diversities and Diversities creates Developments in direct, indirect and induced ways. It has multiplier effect on the economy and natural environment.

2. *Humanity, Harmony and Human Innovation (3H):* Humanity creates Harmony and Harmony may result in great Human Innovation. Therefore 'H' factor becomes important while developing strategies and policies for migration, migrants, immigrants and Diasporas as Home Country (origin) or Host Country (residing). No development can sustain in lack of these Hs.

3. *Approach, Appreciation and Alignment (3A):* Over the years, Diasporas have played a traditional, albeit consistent role in contributing to their homelands' economies through increasingly large levels of remittances. Most recently, they also have begun to represent a unique human resource that comprises specific knowledge, experience, and enthusiasm that can be organized productively to assist with a variety of development initiatives back home. In addition to contributing to their home countries' economic development (through the provision of financial and/or material resources), Diasporas constitute a wealth of skilled and qualified manpower that can be tapped into for other areas of development – i.e., forging partnerships to address issues surrounding health, education, civil society, democracy and governance, conflict mitigation, etc.

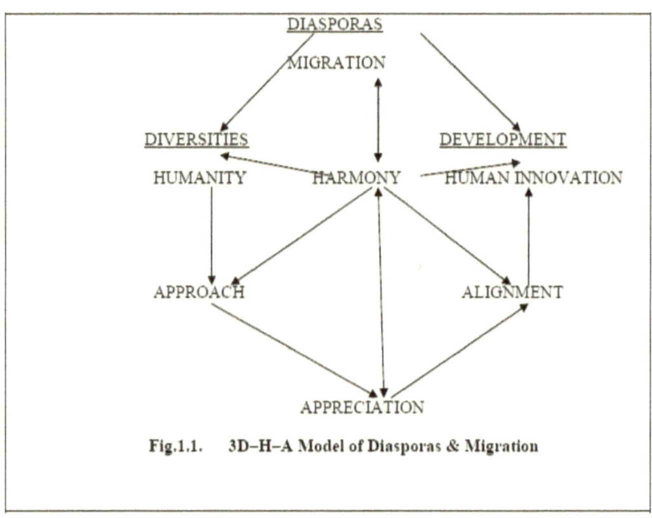

Fig.1.1.   3D–H–A Model of Diasporas & Migration

Individuals in a Diaspora are often considered to be consolidated into a somewhat cohesive group, despite the fact that many typically do not hold a single homogenous identity. In theory, the groups are a manifestation of numerous identities – ethnic, political, religious, generational, and/or otherwise – that coalesces and, due to an overarching affiliation to its homeland, integrate into homogenous Diasporic identities (Ogden, 2008). Differentiation within the groups, however, appears to be the norm – for instance, in terms of political affiliation, economic status, etc. As a result, Diasporic communities are multifaceted.

Despite the contextual nature of Diasporic identities, these groups remain a constructive, yet underutilized, resource within the international development arena. The so-called "Diaspora Option" – also called the "Diaspora Approach" or co-development – is the utilization of expatriate individuals and groups as catalysts in the implementation of development programs in their home countries, and has become a growing trend.

All the above three dimensional factors (3D, 3H, 3A) lased with three different elements are vital to come out with any conclusion.

Diasporas of any country should not be kept aside from mainstream work and political know how or understanding. Only engagement of diasporas in day to day activities and participation in knowledge, technology transfer and innovation by providing them more rights socially and politically would help in the growth and development of any region, state or nation.

The country like USA has grown more fast than in comparison to any other country because of proper utilization of their diasporas and flexible visa policy for immigration. China has also opened its door for big companies but its immigration policy has been exceptional in the world. Of course when you opened the door for migration or immigration the impact could be positive or negative but consideration should be more on positive side than negative.

Diasporas can bring change in the economy of any country, if it is treated as boon instead of burden.

SCOPE FOR DIASPORAS TOURISM

Although a significant percentage of immigrants visit their home countries as tourists, typically, there is still no tourism policy aimed at diasporas. The lack of such policy reflects government neglect and is a lost opportunity. Governments and the private sector can participate in joint ventures to offer their diasporas tour packages to visit traditional and non-traditional sites to rediscover and discover their home countries. They can also work out investment alliances with diasporas interested in partnering to establish joint ventures relating to tourism.

Diasporas Tourism

The scope of Diaspora Tourism is very high as it is still untapped areas of tourism that can be linked with "*Virtual Tourism*" as well. Diasporas has been playing a great role in the development of their country of origin as well as host country where they reside. These Diasporas particularly settled in abroad with dual citizenship or single citizenship of residing country is the major market for tourism sector. They are very eager to see their roots in their country of origin like ancestral house, village, culture, fair, festival, food etc. Country like India has tremendous scope in such areas. Destination Management Organisation needs to promote "Diasporas Tourism" in collaboration with overseas tour operators and travel agents. The concerned government also needs to design certain framework in collaboration with tourism departments and organisation to offer suitable package of tourism to satisfy the need of Diasporas in their native country. Attracting Diasporas through tourism would not only bring prosperity but also help in improving basic infrastructures and superstructures in the country. Diaspora can provide their valuable inputs in various areas of tourism.

*For example, the leisure tourism market in Africa represents over half of the international tourist arrivals to Africa and is characterized by high-end trips to top wildlife watching and nature destinations, niche tourism products such as adventure trips and cultural heritage tours and lower-end beach holidays. The middle-income market on the other hand remains relatively underdeveloped. The most established tourism products in Africa are safari, beach resort, business and **Diaspora tourism** while newly emerging products are adventure tourism (mainly nature-related such as trekking and adventure sports), cultural heritage and wellness/health tourism(UNWTO Report,2015).*

Virtual Tourism can be used as catalyst to attract the Diasporas through various web based application on tourist place, historical place, village, city, people, costume, ethnic food, fairs, festival, dance, music, etc. on internet. And once this system of virtual tourism becomes able to generate want, then next responsibility of DMO is to convert it into" need".

Concerned government must give tax holiday and other benefits to Diasporas during their journey, visit and stay to their country of origin.

Separate channel for exit and entry need to be designed for such tourists with traditional welcoming procedures beginning from airport itself.

Expert Guide must be provided to such group and special attention needs to be taken in terms of safety and security. It doesn't mean that other foreigner tourists should be ignored from all such facilities.

Special provision should be there to facilitate fast MoU(Memorandum of Understanding) process on the spot regarding any project or venture for which diasporas have shown interest.

Diasporas Children or Dependents exchange programmes can be one of the attractive options for facilitating short term tourism for long term gain as it matters a lot in taking decision.

SUGGESTIVE FRAMEWORK

1. Role or contribution of Diasporas in country of residence/work

Diasporas - Diversities -Challenges - Opportunities -Innovations- Growth - Development(Socio-Economic) - Satisfaction (Among People)- Peace & Prosperity

*(-) means creates /generates

2. Role of Diasporas for country of origin

Diasporas = Money(Remittance) + Globalisation(Culture) = Growth +Development = Peace +Prosperity

*Establishing Diaspora International Cooperative Banks (DICB) in respective villages of Diasporas to motivate diaspora to facilitate all round support to growth and development their native villages.

* Opening of business centres, skill development centres, etc. on the name of respective Diasporas.

*Yearly award to best diaspora communities.

And for getting success in regard to above strategic model following things need to be followed,

More importantly, donors and other international organizations, such as the United Nations and the World Bank, should redouble their efforts to solve the "last mile" problem, and in partnership with the private sector assure that even in the most remote locations of the globe there is access to the Internet. Without proper sustainable channels of communications (radio, TV, Internet) to nurture the sharing and transfer of information and knowledge, the billions of dollars being spent today on fighting AIDS, other diseases, famine, illiteracy, poverty and in salvaging the environment are, in a sense, being dissipated. Without a constant flow of information and knowledge to nurture these development initiatives, they will wither and die.

The granting of dual citizenship is a significant measure adopted by home countries to formalize the belonging of their Diasporas to the home country, both in a symbolic and concrete way. Several home countries grant dual citizenship with a view to facilitating diaspora contributions.

The right to buy land and property appears to be another powerful incentive for instance, eliminated sales tax on property transactions and offered subsidized interest rates for the acquisitions of properties by diaspora members.

The World Bank (2005) emphasizes the significance of portable social security benefits, in particular pension and health benefits. However, this portability is usually achieved through bilateral social security agreements between the sending and the receiving countries, and targets in particular temporary labour migrants.

Acknowledge the diversity of diaspora interests and strategies :- allowing diasporas to choose the contributions they wished to make.

Allow Diasporas to keep ownership of their initiatives and contributions

Establish collaboration between home and host countries:- Both integration policies in the host country and pro-diaspora policies of the home country raise issues of social inclusion and belonging. This questions Diasporas' double allegiance to the host and the home country, and potential frictions between the inclusion in the host society and the belonging to a diaspora identity.

Match diaspora resources with genuine development needs and facilitate cooperation between diasporas and existing development institutions (investment projects, microcredits, mutual funds) and innovative development practices (business incubators, clusters of enterprises, social enterprises, women networks, business services, activities of chambers of commerce, training, etc).

Support the participation of Diasporas in partnerships with the private sector, academia, the public sector (hospitals, schools, etc.), international organizations, NGOs, recruitment agencies, business development services or chambers of commerce that can relate diaspora inputs to identified development needs.

Adopt incentives that will attract Diasporas to participate in development programmes.

Identify the obstacles that Diasporas perceive as barriers to their contributions: lack of an appropriate transport or banking infrastructure, bureaucratic burdens, weak partnerships, corruption, lack of support networks, unclear interlocutors at governmental level, poor consular services, etc.

CONCLUSION

Diasporas can bring change in the economy of any country, if it is treated as boon instead of burden. Establishment of *Diaspora International Cooperative Banks* (DICB) in respective villages of Diasporas to motivate diaspora to facilitate all round support to growth and development of Diaspora's native villages. Promotion of Diasporas tourism by implementing the suggestive framework and monitoring the process as per 3D-H-A Model of Diaspora and Migration may lead to success story. Proper policy frameworks need to be developed by each country for the best suit of their Diasporas.

REFERENCES

- Appadurai, A. (1990) 'Disjuncture and Difference in the Global

Cultural Economy'. In M. Featherstone (ed.) *Global Culture: Nationalism, Globalization and Modernity.* London: Sage, pp.295-310.

- Basch, L., Glick Schiller, N. and Szanton Blanc, C. (1994) *Nations Unbound: Transnational*

- Brinkerhoff, Jennifer M. 2003. Digital Diasporas and International Development: Afghan-Americans and the Reconstructions of Afghanistan. The GW Center for the Study of Globalization, Occasional Paper Series. http://gstudynet.org/publications/OPS/papers/CSGOP-03-23.pdf.

- Clifford, J. (1988) *The Predicament of Culture: Twentieth-Century Ethnography, Literature and Art.* Cambridge, Mass.: Harvard University Press.

- Clifford, J. (1992) 'Traveling Cultures'. In L. Grossberg, C. Nelson and P. A. Treichler (eds.) *Cultural Studies.* New York: Routledge. pp. 96-116.

- De Haas, H. (2006, June). Emerging diasporas: How governments and development agencies can support diaspor involvement in the development of origin countries. International Migration Institute. James Martin 21st Century School. University of Oxford.

- Diminescu D (2008). The connected migrant: an epistemological manifesto. *Social Science Information, 47*. 565-579.

- Dina Ionescu, 2006, Engaging Diasporas as Development Partners for Home and Destination Countries: Challenges for Policymakers, International Organization for Migration, Geneva

- Duque, R. (2008). Is the Internet accelerating brain drain and brain waste or is it creating opportunities for brain gain and brain circulation? *Conference Papers -- American Sociological Association, 1-17.*

- Ernst, D. (2008, February). Can Chinese IT firms develop innovative capabilities within global knowledge networks? East-West Center Working Papers. No. 94.

- Faist, T. (1997) 'International Migration and Transnational Social Spaces: The Turkish-German Example'. Paper presented at the Third Conference of the European Sociological Association, University of Essex, UK, 25 - 30 August 1997.

- Featherstone, M. (ed.) (1990) *Global Culture: Nationalism, Globalization and Modernity.* London: Sage.

- Fontaine, Thomas., Tracing the Diaspora's Involvement in the Development of a Nation: The Case of Dominica. Prepared for the George Washington University's Research Workshop and Edited Book Project on: The Role of Diasporas in Developing the Homeland. http://www.thedominican.net/articl es/diasporaPaper.pdf

- Girma, B. (2007). Report shows brain drain cost country dearly. *The Africa Monitor.* April 29,2007. Available at: http://74.125.93.132/search?q=cac

he:http://www.theafricamonitor.co
m/news/ethiopian/april2007/2904
07/report.htm

- Gueron, J. and Spevacek, A. M. (2008). Diaspora-development nexus: The role of ICT. USAID Knowledge Services Center. Available at: http://www.unitar.org/ny/sites/def ault/files/Hannafin%20ICT%20Dias poras.pdf

- Gupta, A. and Ferguson, J. (1992) 'Beyond "Culture": Space, Identity, and the Politics of Difference'. *Cultural Anthropology,* 7, 6-23.

- Hall, S. (1991) 'The Local and the Global: Globalization and Ethnicity'. In A. D. King (ed.) *Culture, Globalization and the World-System.* London: Macmillan, pp. 19-39.

- http://www.chileglobal.org/. Chile Global is an international network of Chilean business owners and top level executives living abroad, who have an interest in contributing to Chile's economic development.

- IADB-MIF. "RG-M1019: MIF-IFAD Partnership Facility for Rural Private Sector Dev-LAC." Available at: http://www.iadb.org/projects/Project.cfm?project=RG-M1019&Language=English. 2006a. Accessed July 18, 2007.

- Indian Diaspora(ICT) - includes Intel, Oracle, Sun Microsystems, Texas Instruments, and IBM.

- Joseph Gueron, M/CIO/KM Division Chief, Anne Marie Spevacek, M/CIO/KM/KSC Senior Research Analyst, 2008,Diaspora-Development Nexus: The Role Of ICT, USAID

- Kearney, M. (1995) 'The Local and the Global: The Anthropology of Globalization and Transnationalism'. *Annual Review of Anthropology,* 24, 547-565.

- Lowell, B. Lindsay and Stefka G. Gerova. September 2004. Diasporas and Economic Development: State of Knowledge. Washington, DC: Institute for the Study of International Migration. Paper prepared for the World Bank.

http://siteresources.worldbank.org/
INTGEP2006/Resources/LowellDias
pora.doc.

- Massey, Douglas S., Adela Pellegrino, J. Edward Taylor, Ali Kouaouci, Joaquin Arango, and Graeme Hugo. 1999. Worlds in Motion: Understanding International Migration at the End of the Millennium. New York: Oxford University Press.

- Multilateral Investment Fund (MIF). Receptores de remesas en Bolivia, Peru. Washington, DC: Washington, DC, Mulitalateral Investment Fund of the Inter-American Development Bank, September 2005.

- Newland, Kathleen, and Hiroyuki Tanaka. 2010. *Mobilizing Diaspora Entrepreneurship for Development.* Washington, DC: Migration Policy Institute

- Orozco, Manuel. "International Flows of Remittances: Cost, competition and financial access in Latin America and the Caribbean—toward an industry scorecard." Report presented at the meeting on

"Remittances and Transnational Families" sponsored by the Multilateral Fund of the Inter-American Development Bank and the Annie E Casey Foundation, organized on May 12th, 2006a.

- *Projects, Postcolonial Predicaments and Deterritorialized Nation-States.* Basel: Gordon & Breach.

- Robertson, R. (1995) 'Glocalization: Time-Space and Homogeneity-Heterogeneity'. In M. Featherstone, S. Lash and R. Robertson (eds.) *Global Modernities.* London: Sage, pp. 25-44.

- Robinson, Jenny. 2002. Development and Displacement. Oxford: Oxford University Press.

- Saxenian, A. (2003). Brain circulation and capitalist dynamics: The Silicon Valley-Hsinchu-Shanghai Triangle. The Center for Economy and Society. CSES Working Paper Series. Paper # 8.

- Saxenian, A. (2007). *The New Argonauts: Regional Advantage in a*

Global Economy. Harvard University Press.

- Tung, R. (2008). Brain circulation, diaspora, and international competitiveness. *European Management Journal, 26*(5). 298-304.

- Turner, W. A. (2003). Diaspora knowledge networks. ICCSSD.

- UNDP. Human Development Report 2006. Beyond Scarcity: Power, Poverty, and the Global Water Crisis. New York: UN Development Programme, 2006. Available at: http://hdr.undp.org/hdr2006/stati stics/indices/tools.cfm. Accessed June 11, 2007.

- Wahlbeck, Ö. (1998) 'Community Work and Exile Politics: Kurdish Refugee Associations in London'. *Journal of Refugee Studies,* 11, No. 3.

- Waters, M. (1995) *Globalization.* London: Routledge

- World Bank (2010). *Global Economic Prospects: Crisis, Finance and Growth.* Washington, DC.

- http://www.unifem.org/prfiles/4/1 KAMPALA Declaration.pdf

- http://cit.aed.org/forecast sudan.htm

- http://www.geekcorps.org/category /programs/snadd/

- http://www.ethiopiandiaspora.org

- http://www.armeniadiaspora.com/

- http://www.unicttaskforce.org/stak eholders/ddn.html

- http://go.worldbank.org/HT1YT23N S0

- http://tofa.af/

- http://www.starradio.org.lr/content /view/481/27/http://uite.org/cms /index.php

- http://www.dfid.gov.uk/news/files/ support-dispora-volunteers.asp

- http://www.unesco.org/shs/migrati on/diaspora http://www.unesco.org/education/ studyingabroad/highlights/braindra in

- http://www.iom.int/MIDA/

- http://www.atpac.org/atpac
  2003/index.htm

CHAPTER 9

EMERGING FORMS OF TOURISM AND ITS ADJECTIVAL: INVADERS OR AMBASSADOR

Emerging areas of tourism and its adjectival has emerged as dynamic factors that may boost the nations' economy and can give diversified impact on socio cultural aspect of tourism. The tourism is also measured as unit of economic growth of a particular zone, state, and in some country. Therefore tourism should not promote enclave and cruise ship tourism which leads to economic leakages. The new adjectival of tourism has both positive and negative dimensions and therefore negative dimensions must also be considered to prevent future problems due to new forms of tourism. The present chapter focuses on both negative and positive side of tourism and its dimension. The chapter is based on discussion with eminent scholars, experts, historians, and professionals. It provides a suitable framework to meet with contingencies. And also explain about importance of Relationship Management to run a micro entrepreneur.

INTRODUCTION

The emerging areas of tourism and manipulated adjectival of tourism that has both positive and negative side and which is also a matter of serious concern to avoid anti tourism activities from host communities in future. Tourism should not be cause of panic for communities or society otherwise it would be terrible and disaster for tourist/guest communities. The promotion of tourism should not be on playing human emotions, sentiments and carrying capacity of destination. Ecological balance and cultural value need to be considered while planning, designing, packaging and selling the product. Tourism is not to invade the indigenous culture, traditions and moral value of local communities, however it may help in eradication of rooted and an age old superstition but that too steadily. Preservation and conservation of all the pulling factor of destination and sustainable growth spreading through peace and prosperity must be the ultimate aim of tourism phenomenon. The development and promotion of tourism must be within specified dimension and its adjectival (forms) have to follow the dimensions otherwise beyond boundary it is doom-gloom. Dimensions may consist of its culture, ecology, biodiversity, cuisines, art and craft, religion, language, climate, occupation, tradition, class, caste, natural resources, man- made resources, mythology.

Tourism is for connecting people, not neglecting people. It is one of the powerful driver as well as stimulator of economy particularly for country like India. The negative dimension and changing form of tourism such as Doomsday, Terror tourism, Dark tourism and other such type of emerging for will ruin the positive side of tourism. Therefore attention must be given in creating new form considering its positive impact in long term.

Through tourism not only we can promote the small scale industries but also micro entrepreneurs. By bringing tourist closer to host community scope of economic development in that are increased which further leads into the direction of poverty eradication and employment generation. It would not only bring foreign currency through service and export of indigenous materials in overseas but also brings happiness in the life of host communities or country.

Tourism is a kind of RM (Relationship Management) based approach whether that relationship is related with nature, environment, wild life, art & draft, monuments, garden, beaches, mountains, streams, river or with local community and their age old cultural heritage. In any case tourism has to form relationship to survive in long term. Managing hormonal relationship with all the important factors, constituents and beneficiaries to lead the sustainable form of responsible tourism must be the ultimate goal of any tourism related activities. Not a single element should be remained untouched.

Creativity and innovativeness is important in all sectors but it should not been on the ground on cultural, moral, and emotional sacrifices of the local community and their interest. Tourism must innovate new dimensions but through measuring its impact on the emotions, sentiments and moral of local people in which it is being flourished or going to be flourished. In the process of creation new form of tourism and practice creator should never forget the impact in future. The purpose of tourism must be in right proportion of moral, emotion, perception and sentiments of local community.

TOURISM DYNAMICS

Priscilla Boniface (2001) in his book titled dynamics of tourism represents a journey of exploration that is personal and which is in some way an odyssey. The book explains about dynamic tourism means doing tourism differently. On the one hand concern is wide spread about the potential for damage from tourism. Tourism can have harmful social, cultural and environmental effects. On the other hand, as a tool for change tourism is widely seen as a chance for social, cultural and economic benefits. Tourism can solve problems offering new development in some places, regeneration in others. It insight into dynamic relationship in between the host societies, the target sites, their visitors and the tourism industry itself. It is clear that education and training are central to achieving a general understanding that change is required in tourism. Needs and reason of change must be communicated.

C. Michael Hall & Williams Allan (2008), tourism is often described as an industry with high growth rates, and it is subject to radical change in how it is produced and consumed. However, there is still a relatively poor understanding of how such changes are brought about – that is, through innovation. This book is the first to provide a comprehensive review of innovation in tourism, while also considering how tourism itself contributes to innovative local, regional and national development strategies.

Mike Robinson & Priscilla Boniface (1999), Tourism can revive local economies, preserve cultures, and even resurrect lost traditions. However, it can also result in conflicts with existing values, economic relations, social norms, and traditions, sometimes resulting in pervasive or violent resistance. This book examines the changing relationships between tourism and host cultures and explores how and why conflicts emerge.

Mowferth ,1998, Increasingly, advocates of tourism argue that tourism growth offers a means for third World countries to escape the confines of 'underdevelopment' and that new forms of tourism in particular allow this transition to be achieved sustainably and equitably. Building upon this fundamental precept, explores and challenges the notions of sustainability, globalization and development, and their relationship to contemporary tourism in the third World.

Adopting a broad geographical and conceptual perspective, clear understanding of the tourism process and its relationship to development can only be achieved by an interdisciplinary approach, touching on environmentalism, socio-cultural studies, human geography, economics and development studies.

KEY POINTS NEED TO BE ADDRESSED IN TOURISM

- Cultural and other tourism promotional activities may be boost up to foster tourism.

- Change is always appreciated, tourism is synonym to it but every change brings along pros and con so welcome change.

- Lots of adjectival (forms) of tourism will spoil the recipe of tourism.

- Policy makers should promote Tourism in such a way that it should go beyond the economic aspects.

GLOBALIZATION OF TOURISM AND HOSPITALITY SECTOR

Globalization has given a diversified and variable impact on the growth and development of its fundamental components and motivational factors. Due to globalization cultures, cuisines, customs, credibility and concept (5Cs) components of tourism has been shifting from destination to destination. And due to which nowadays it has become difficult to find and feel the authenticity of pulling factors. Tourists and guests are confused in selecting right products and have been facing problem in differentiating in between original and duplicate. Even sometime he/she feels comfortable with duplicate product and they feel to be cheated with original products. Due to globalization market is full of fake things.

Further depending on practice of tourism in other country and trying to implement in country like India has no logic. India and its rich diversity can't be compared with any of the country of this world. India is a basket of different types of flowers in terms of cultural, religious, cuisines, traditions, and biodiversity. Indian is unique and its resources are incomparable. India has some issues and challenges on cultural & religious differences but that is there everywhere in different parts of the world even though they are single religion dominant country. Globalization is good but after certain extent it needs to be stopped.

MIU (Marketing Intelligence Unit)

Every state should concentrate on conservation of rich cultural heritage, tradition, cuisine, environment and ecology of their area which is precious if they would like to be benefited from tourism and hospitality.

RELATIONSHIP MANAGEMENT- helps in building trust among local people as well as in surrounding.

For example: Micro Entrepreneurs: an owner of tea centre for livelihood in Ahmedabad.

A tea centre in a village locality is being managed by regular customers, auto drivers, shop keeper and other trust worthy persons in absentia of owner in a courteous way to serve the clients. Most important aspect of this small tea centre is diversified services and assistance. It prepares tea as per demand and taste of customers that makes it more unique in terms of size and dimensions. Customers are satisfied. I am also a customer of this tea centre. Such type of models may be created in respect of other occupations.

As far as micro entrepreneurship in catering and hotel related businesses are concerned, scope and future of hotel industry is very bright particularly for developing country like India. As of now only 30 % women force are engaged in service including of business. And in future this is definitely going to increase due to rising inflation and changing working culture. It would be supported by friendly work environment for females and favourable conditions from their family members due to changing perception in cultural, moral and ethical values among people. A globalization thrust will compel people to redefine their values in more scientific and systematic way rather than classical ways to meet their essential and desirable needs.

The new era in future will be future of apartment, residential and semi-residential hotels which will further dominated by micro entrepreneurs. We can project the aforesaid change to be effective in next 25 years i.e. upto year 2040. Dynamic approaches of people will facilitate economic growth in which Relationship Management would be versatile driver.

Tourism and hospitality industry will push the economy of any nation particularly to developing nations.

EMERGING FORMS TOURISM (positive or negative)

Tourism that can sustain for longer duration and may result in positive or negative impact are;

(i) Cruise tourism – Cruise tourism will capture the market in coming days because it would be a kind of great destination for recreation, relaxation and adventure for tourist, traveler and explorer. India tourism has also focused on creating new circuits of cruise tourism.

(ii)Casino Tourism- casino going to be popular in coming days particularly in country like India where demand would be more in coming days.

(iii) Sports Tourism -sports tourism has tremendous scope in the world and can be developed with indigenous and age old traditional sports like Chess (Satranj), Kabaddi, Hockey, and other games like Gilli Danda rather than on foreign invaded games. Cricket, Football and Golf has already attracted a large number of tourists from different parts of the world.

(iv) Traditional Textile Tourism (TTT) - hundreds type of traditional clothing around the world and looms, weavers life need to be focused and visited during such type of tourism activities. It focuses on indigenous traditional manufacturing methods and showcases the lifestyles of weavers.

(v) **Wine Tourism** – people would like to see vineyard, field and the production methods of wine, its tasting.

(vi) **Gay Tourism** – is also going to emerge as a form of tourism to fulfill the demand of homosexual aspect.

(vii)**Art and Craft Tourism-** 100 types of art and craft, craftsman, manufacturing methods, life styles, environment, their culture and food need to be promoted through tourism.

(viii)**Garden Tourism**- searching gardens and visitors for its uniqueness which is thousand years old may be organised and showcased through such type of tourism.

(ix) **Ethnic Tourism** –that promotes indigenous lifestyles, dignity of culture and traditions.

(x) **Spice village Tourism** – food lovers and herbal medicine experts have been taking interest in visiting such villages or farm where different variety of spices are produced.

(xi)**Wooden Architecture Tourism** - hundred and thousand years old architecture need to be defined and tourist must need to be motivated to visit such place through showcasing.

(xii)**Trade Tourism** -new form of tourism may evolve due to rapid expansion of tourism businesses and movement of people throughout the world. The reason of this will be globalization and people inclination towards finding diversified source of income to meet with inflation as well as competition related issues.

(xiii) **Doom tourism**-Termed 'last-chance' or 'doom' tourism in the popular media, the desire for tourists to witness vanishing landscapes or seascapes and disappearing species.

(xiv) **Doomsdays**-Tourists flocking to Guatemala for "end of the world". Seeing it before you can't. It includes places, ceremonies, procession, places, monuments, island, species, studying games and tools such as flashcards.

(xv) **Virtual Tourism**- has emerged as a new form of tourism among the techno savvy people have shortage of time but more discretionary income and 24 X 7 internet connection on latest gadgets. An emerging area of research in "Techno-tourism".

Q. Is Virtual Tourism going to fill the gap of tourism or to kill the conventional tourism system/phenomenon?

Technology is good to boost the growth of tourism and to increase the impact of visualization by providing more tangible experience through projection of facts, figure, pictures, videos to aspiring tourist/visitors/drifters/explorers/natural ist, but at the same time killing the originality and authenticity of tourism products and its process. It would give impact in different dimensions i.e. socio-economic, physical and experiential...But again it's an untapped area that needs to be discussed and explored to bring it in more positive than negative.

(xvi) **Terror Tourism** :- such type of tourism provides opportunity to see the places of terror attacks and its impact.

TRENDS AND SUGGESTIONS

The new form of tourism will provide bigger dimensions to tourism.

Failures only prove out that efforts have not been given from bottom of heart in right direction. And at the same time a failure provide opportunity to gain experience and provides scope of new funda of business to start with.

More demand would be for nature based tourism but it does not mean that culture based tourism will die, that will also continue.

In country where more availability of impulsive travellers (not planned their travel in proper way, it suddenly happens). Home stay is also not going to survive in some countries as in these countries culture is more affected with myth and biases. Such people feel insulted when someone or neighbour questioned for homestay in regard to loosing dignity in society or communities as they treat outsiders as invaders unless it is defined that they are family guest. Group size has been also reducing day by day due to less participation of cultural, traditional and ethnic components in tourism activities. The country has been moving towards multinational slavery which produces mental slavery.

TOURISM MODEL FOR RURAL GROWTH

Villages are the unit of national integration and world formation. Villages are different from each other in terms of culture, religion, moral values, caste, cult, sect, cuisines, fairs, festivals, language, art and craft and in terms of various other dimensions. There are some villages which are near to urban areas, whereas some are in remotest locations. Many villages have limited resources and potential in terms of tourism development but on the other hand many have tremendous potential to adopt the tourism as a part of their livelihood.

Now the first thing which we can do is to find out the framework of modeling the village.

1. Identification of all the villages in a country.

2. Categorisation of list of village into (i) Remotest (ii) Remote (iii) Sub urban (iv) Urban Village

3. Starting with remotest first and then entered into other respective category of village

4. Ministry of Tourism should integrate all the manpower development institute imparting education & training in the tourism stream.

5. Making compulsory for every student to serve minimum one village and maximum 5 village during the tenure (allocation of minimum and maximum number of village modeling will depend upon duration of course) of their course.

6. This will also help in job security of students for time being and utilization of innovativeness and creativity.

6. Modeling of village would depend upon feasibility study and sustainability of residing community.

7. Mentor must be allotted to each one of these village who may be a faculty or professionals.

8. Big and small corporate houses to be motivated and anticipated in project modeling.

9. Corporate Social Responsibility need to be redefined in terms of mentorship in such activities.

10. If required a philanthropic society can be formed to use the accrued amount from corporate houses or individuals who are the part of this philanthropic society. And there must be provision of special tax holiday scheme for contributing to such type of activities from government side so that it could connect more donors.

11. Financial Institution must be motivated to participate.

12. Villages rich and well established in tourism and entrepreneurship must be invited to contribute their ideas for new projects.

13. Conferences, workshops, trade shows must be organized for new village participant to familiarize with benefits of tourism and other economic activities.

14. Without hampering the religious beliefs, moral values and prestige, modeler should interpret the impact of tourism and other economic activities and how these activities will bring change in their life style.

Ever country has different issues and challenge but out of all major challenge is religion, caste and cultural values with which people don't want to compromise. They take outside people as invaders instead of ambassador . Therefore every modelers and mentors must keep in his/her mind that they have to build an understanding approach of tourism concepts and must have ability or diplomacy to transform people(community's) psychology regarding tourist/guest/visitors from invaders to ambassador .

Modelers and mentors must try to form a network by adding people through individual and group counselling but keeping in mind that moral & cultural values are intact. Awareness must be generated in such a way so that people of residing areas will feel proud in tourism promotion and could become a question of prestige in those villages who ignored the importance of tourism.

CONCLUSION

Tourism can have harmful social, cultural and environmental effects. On the other hand, as a tool for change tourism is widely seen as a chance for social, cultural and economic benefits. Tourism can solve problems offering new development in some places, regeneration in others. It insight into dynamic relationship in between the host societies, the target sites, their visitors and the tourism industry itself. It is clear that education and training are central to achieving a general understanding that change is required in tourism. Needs and reason of change must be communicated. However, there is still a relatively poor understanding of how such changes are brought about – that is, through innovation. Adopting a broad geographical and conceptual perspective, clear understanding of the tourism process and its relationship to development can only be achieved by an interdisciplinary approach, touching on environmentalism, socio-cultural studies, human geography, economics and development studies.

REFERENCES

- Priscilla Boniface, 2001,Dynamic Tourism: Journeying With Change, Channel View Publications .

- C. Michael Hall & Williams Allan (2008),Tourism And Innovation, Routledge

- By Mike Robinson & Priscilla Boniface,1999, Tourism And Cultural Conflicts, Oxford University Press

- Mowferth,1998, Tourism And Sustainability: New Tourism In The Third World, Routledge 1998, London

(page purposely kept blank)

CHAPTER 10

SPIRITUAL HOLIDAY ECO-TOURISM: PERSPECTIVE OF SAARC Nations

Spiritual Holiday Eco-Tourism (SHET) has been looked upon in different dimensions since the inception of the word "tourism" on this human dominated earth which is full of sorrows, frustrations, selfishness, and affected by blind development of science and technology knowingly or unknowingly its consequences. New travel patterns reflect changes in consumer behaviour, economic strength of source markets, new destinations, and political realignments. Shifts to North-South tourist flows are occurring in Asia (towards ASEAN countries, Australia and the Pacific Islands.) Community interest and tourism must work together for any chance of long term success. In long term, it is not useful to have isolated tourist enclaves. The most rewarding forms of tourism are those that involve both residents and tourists. "Rewarding" means both in terms of the visitor and resident experiences and the economic viability to the developer. The Chapter reaches on the conclusion that small business development opportunities, not just jobs, will be an increasingly important element of the community benefit package. The tourism industry should encourage and promote entrepreneurship and privatization particularly at the local level.

INTRODUCTION

Spiritual Holiday Eco-Tourism (SHET) has been looked upon in different dimensions since the inception of the word "tourism" on this human dominated earth which is full of sorrows, frustrations, selfishness, and affected by blind development of science and technology knowingly or unknowingly its consequences.

When we look upon the reasons behind the phenomenon of tourism and its forms, we come to know that it is people who have coined it (the word" tourism") for getting pleasure by adopting change in their routine life styles. It was all unexpectedly happened over the period of time and that too for the sake of calmness, tranquility, enjoyment, cure, devotions, spiritual odyssey and friendliness with nature. They never ever thought that the tourism of today would take the form of business in future. The earlier people celebrated the changes (tourism) in a colorful and wonderful way keeping in view the availability of natural resources and its importance in the existence of their life and disaster management as per their present conditions and future requirements. During the period of early settlement of human life, people had deep faith and trust in nature and making relationships which was vanished during the course of time in looking for short cuts and getting one time pleasure. It is all suppressed in fast forward growth and development of infrastructures as well as superstructures for "nine days wonder".

Even today, people of different tribes have deep concerned about natural resources because they live in the lap of beautiful nature. They have also taken learning lessons from the previous phenomenal changes in their surroundings due to disobediences of nature eco system. And that's why learning from the past they follow all the principles while doing traditional ceremonies, festivals, fairs and fulfilling the physiological needs i.e. food, water, cloths and shelters. They are happy with their life styles and they don't want any kind of interference. Perhaps, it is us who think that they are uneducated and in the process of making them educated we leave ample opportunities for them to misinterpret the current affairs of this fast moving world. Results of those misinterpretations and mismanagement we can see now in the form of natural calamities, cold war, terrorism, disrupting peace, prosperity and consensus in the SAARC regions.

Spiritual Holiday Tourism has contributed a great role in the development of World tourism apart from other common types of tourism such as leisure, adventure, health, business incentive, special interest, wildlife, educational etc.

Tourism is now a well-known sector, which has power to change the economy of any country in this world. International tourism industry has 10.2 per cent share of the global GDP with 10.6 per cent of the global force being engaged in tourism. India has 0.4 per cent share of world tourism, which is very less as per tourism potentiality of India (WTTC).

Spiritual Holiday Eco- Tourism (SHET) can be one of the effective and emerging form of tourism that has power to safeguard the interests of tourists and hosts, which will further help in strengthening the economy and inter-relationships of South Asian countries for establishing peace, prosperity and consensus regarding the promotion of eco-friendly tourism as well as formulation of strategies. By putting hands together in order to spread peace and awareness through tourism and getting benefits out of its impacts in the SAARC region we may preserve the rich cultural heritage, natural resources and the whole eco-system.

The main objective of this research paper is to find out the new emerging form of tourism and its possibility to satisfy and cater the regional needs from the grass root level and how to unite for peace and prosperity on the basis of tourism promotion. There are so many things which is common in between all these countries and we need to focus on those things. The inspiration is taken from "Lotus" the flower that has no religion but can be used for all.

Lotus flowers are amazing and have great spiritual significance and strong symbolic ties to many South Asian religions. Lotus signified for its delicate beauty, but mostly because it expresses the qualities that we want in our life, both spiritually and practically. Spiritually the lotus symbolises new beginnings, enlightenment, divine beauty, and honour. On a practical level every single part of a lotus can be used, there is no need for any wastage - the petals, stamens, seeds, young leaves, stems, and rhizomes are all edible, whilst the larger older leaves are used as a food wrapping.

The main objective of this research paper is how to promote Spiritual Holiday Eco-Tourism (SHET) as per the carrying capacity of particular destination by minimizing the amount of natural wastage and maximizing the beauty with empowering the local inhabitants. The environmental degradation should be stopped today otherwise tomorrow will be too late for everybody. The lotus flower acts as inspirational source for the sustainable development of Tourism in the region. This study has come out with a suitable models and master plan for the region.

Spiritual Holiday Tourism – is a process of attaining personal odyssey through the outer reaches of beliefs for getting metal and physical satisfaction. Spiritual Holiday destinations are the land of wonderful experiences to satisfy the mind, body heart and soul. The Spiritual Tourist is an odyssey through many of the religious and spiritual groups, traditions and happenings which are a marked feature of the contemporary world. Even miracles were being claimed by some of the tourists who had witnessed this phenomenon. Yoga, meditation, rejuvenation, spa, hamam and devotion are major pulling factor that attract people from different part of world towards South Asian country and of course natural beauty always be remained as prime attraction for the promotion of such types of tourism.

Mick Brown (London, Bloomsbury 1999), in his book recounts for number of examples from different part of world such as his visit to Puttaparthi in India where a huge ashram has grown up around the Indian mystic and guru Sathya Sai Baba. He also visits Sera Tibetan Buddhist monastery near Bangalore where he meets a young, Spanish-born lama who is believed to be a tulku – a reincarnation of a previous lama. Again, he travels to Germany to receive darshan – the experience of being in the presence of a guru – from 'Mother Meera' (made famous by Andrew Harvey in his book Hidden Journey). He also visits a church in the Bible Belt of Tennessee where, it was claimed, crosses and angels had suddenly appeared in the window glass.

Eco-Tourism: "Responsible travel to natural areas that conserves the environment and improves the well-being of local people." The International Ecotourism Society (TIES, 1990)

PRINCIPLES OF ECOTOURISM:

Ecotourism is about uniting conservation, communities, and sustainable travel. This means that those who implement and participate in ecotourism activities should follow the following

Eco-tourism principles: Minimize impact.

- Build environmental and cultural awareness and respect.

- Provide positive experiences for both visitors and hosts.

- Provide direct financial benefits for conservation.

- Provide financial benefits and empowerment for local people.

- Raise sensitivity to host countries' political, environmental, and social climate.

Therefore' the combination of above two may result as drastic changes in SAARC region and will provide an ample opportunity to utilize the tourism resources for getting benefits in the form of peace and prosperity out of this sustainable growth and development.

REVIEW OF TOURISM POTENTIAL

Spiritual holiday tourism and Eco-Tourism account for a significant share of international tourist travel, for example to China, Thailand, Japan, and Singapore for their well-managed traditional meditation centres, acupuncture, and herbal treatment to relax body, mind, heart and soul. India is known for its Yoga and Meditations, various Ayurvedic and Yogic treatments. The economic gains are obvious, but there will also be additional demand for infrastructures, professionals and others facilities. This demand could, in turn, lead to further development of suitable sites that has capacity and potentiality to attract tourists i.e. domestic as well as international and could generate revenue and employment to meet with the expectation of concerned Government. In India itself Pilgrimage tourism is one of the important types of tourism, which contributes 40% of total income, which is coming from hospitality and tourism sector.

Spiritual tourism in India has many offerings for world travelers. Whether a tourist seeking rest and relief from the pressures of daily challenges, or looking for answers to religious truths, trying to find the meaning of Life, or on a quest to better understand yourself - or simply wanting to combine the pleasures of traveling to an exotic destination, known for its abiding history of 5000 year old culture, philosophy and secularism with some of the most exciting spiritual holiday for getting peace.

India is a land of inherent spirituality and people have been known to travel here to find solace in its ancient wisdom since time immemorial. India is also the birthplace of the concept of Yoga and Meditation, practices that are becoming increasingly relevant and popular in the context of today's spiritual aridity. Developed by the ancient sage Patanjali in his search for the ultimate unification of the mind, body and spirit with the divine being, or God, Yoga and Meditation are a combination of a series of exercises and mind focusing techniques. They are believed to be the means of achieving 'enlightenment' and 'nirvana.' The verdant valleys and pristine Himalayas of India are the perfect environs for furthering your quest for spirituality.

Some of the most popular Yoga and Meditation tourist destinations in India are the picturesque and peaceful state of Kerala, the spiritual land of Buddha-Bihar, favorite tourist destination for those seeking a cultural heritage tour combined with Yogic instruction is the state of Bihar. Bihar was the home state of the Lord Gautam Buddha, and numerous places associated with different stages of his life, such as Bodhgaya, Sarnath, Kushinagar,

Gaya, Nalanda, etc. are located here. The renowned Bihar School of Yoga at Munger in Bihar offers meditation and yoga sessions for tourists. The pilgrims center of Rishikesh or the quiet and serene town of Dharamshala on the shores of the holy Ganga.

India is rich in biodiversity; it has a vast coastal area having number of beautiful beaches, islands, hill stations, as well as plain area on the bank of holy rivers. It is a land of different cultures, traditions, cuisines, festivals, fairs, languages, costumes and religions as well as a huge number of world heritage sites declared by UNESCO. Indian – a subcontinent sprawling several hundred kilometers, with population over nine hundred million, is undoubtedly the largest democracy in the world with a thousand year old civilization. The project provides an outlook to the various reasons for India being such a sought after tourist destination. Any part of the year India offers a dazzling array of destinations and experiences due to its unique bio-diversity.

Sri Lanka is one of the best places in Asia to spend for Spiritual Holiday Eco-Tourism. Being a religious country, Sri Lanka has a lot many religious places, which attracts tourists from all over the world. Buddhism is the mostly followed religion in Sri Lanka, so most of the pilgrim attractions in Sri Lanka are related to Buddhism. Sri Lanka is one of those places where history seems to fade into the mist of legend. Sri Lanka contains an astonishing seven UNESCO World Heritage Sites within its compact shores. Six cultural sites are testament to a civilization with over 2,000 years of recorded history, while a seventh natural site boasts some of the highest biodiversity found outside the Amazon basin. Experiencing Sri Lanka's heritage sites takes you on a spiritual journey that will uplift and amaze, inspire and refresh.

The major attractions include Temple of Tooth that houses the Sacred tooth relic of Lord Buddha, Sri Pada Peak (Adam's Peak), Dambulla golden temple and Anuradhapura. These religious places are the perfect spots to get some solace and courage and to face the challenges of life. Sri Lanka is a country blessed by nature. Though it is an island, a mere dot on the world map, it is filled with a wide verity of beautiful and ecologically important natural habitats. Sri Lanka is a paradise for animal lovers who enjoy animal or bird watching. There are many national parks and sanctuaries in Sri Lanka that offer you an opportunity to observe "real" wildlife at least once in your lifetime!

Bangladesh has also tremendous potential to explore particularly for Eco-Cultural Tourism. The beautiful and serene beaches of places like Coxs' bazaar that stretch on forever, or a boat journey through the winding, curving backwaters of a Bangladeshi river, with its ancient towns and villages some dating back more than 2000 years, and past maharajas palaces of the previous centuries. It has also a large area of Sunderban covered with different types of flora and fauna.

Pakistan is an extremely hospitable country where visitors are generally treated with great respect. The mighty mountains of Haymalays and Karakuram, the beauty of Thar Desert, The outrageous ocean beaches of karachi, the alluvial plains of punjab make a matchless diversified landscape called Pakistan. The colors of illustrious heritage, the fascination of its deep rooted culture, the insight of centuries old civilizations, the prestige of adventurous trekking and mountaineering and the warmth of hospitality in Pakistan allures thousands of the tourists from around the world yearly.

Nepal and Bhutan has also taken number of initiative to promote tourism as a primary industry and major source of income. A tourism promotion campaign was launched by the government of Nepal at Nanking Darbar Hall, Bangladesh on 5th July with the slogan "Nepal Tourism Year 2011". With an aspiration to expose tourism industry of Nepal, the program was launched by a campaign team of Nepal Tourism Board (NTB) titled "Together for Tourism Year 2011".

TRENDS & CHANGES

Tourism has today achieved the status of peaceful industry and has become more than a cultural pilgrimage. Realizing the various socio-economic benefits of tourism, Government in all countries are competing with each other in selling "tourism & travel" concept its history, culture, sunshine, snow, sands, health treatments, spiritual cure, wildlife and vegetation to people all over the world.

As any economy matures, in the process of development, it makes a transition from agriculture to manufacturing and from manufacturing to services. In different stages of economic growth, the relative importance of these sectors changes in terms of employing people and their relative contribution to GDP. Within the SAARC countries the India sub-continent and Srilanka is well poised to take advantage of the boom in the tourism sector.

The tourism industry is undergoing a sea change with the revolutions in communication and information technology. Everybody in the tourism will have to change and rediscover its place in newly defined value chain. The role and the service offerings will undergo a big change in the present cyber world. Worldwide, Travel & Tourism is expected to grow at a level of 4.0 % per year over the next ten years, creating an opportunity for every country in the world to be part of this process and to share the benefits (WTTC).

Most of India's domestic tourism and inbound tourism is based on Pilgrimage centres. China, Latin America and Commonwealth of Independent States

(CIS) provide lucrative potential markets for the Indian tourism sector, which is poised for greater growth, said the Economic Survey for 2007-08. The survey projected bright prospects for Indian tourism, saying that greater focus needed to be accorded to new emerging markets such China, Latin America and CIS countries.

Sri Lanka seems to be sustainable; tourism to Sri Lanka has a good chance to increase considerably. Mid November at the World Travel Market in London Sri Lanka was called the holiday hit for 2010.

Since the year 2000 tourists arriving in Bangladesh have been swelling in numbers. Many of the visitors are expatriate Bangladeshi coming to Bangladesh not only to visit their families, but for a holiday and to experience the vibrant and culturally rich country of their forbearers. Travelling through Bangladesh is cheap.

Nepal Tourism Board (NTB) recently released a data that showed a 36.6 percent rise in the tourist arrival at the Tribhuvan International Airport (TIA) in March 2010 as compared with the same month last year. The arrivals of visitors from South Asian countries gained a growth of 35.3 percent with increase in Indian tourist by 35.5 percent, Bangladeshis by 53.8 percent, and Pakistanis 3.2 percent. The remarkable rise of tourists was from China with 114 percent in March. Arrivals from Japan, Malaysia and South Korea also saw 6.8 percent, 38.4 percent and 68.1 percent rise respectively. According to NTB, there is 42 percent growth of arrivals from European countries with the arrivals from major countries like UK going up by 44.9 percent, France by 5.4 percent, Germany by 40.8 percent, and Italy by 44 percent and Netherlands by 128.2 percent. Similarly, the tourist arrival from US increased by 6.5 percent, from Canada by 27.2 percent, from Australia by 27.4 percent, and from New Zealand by 69 percent. The implementation of the procedures for home stay facility targeting the foreign visitors is at its final stage. Nepal Tourism Board (NTB) has been working on it to accommodate more visitors in the rural tourist destination.

The 21st century is the century of tourism magic- the most potent weapon of name, fame and reward. Therefore, in the new millennium, SAARC countries need spend millions of dollars for the revamping of the existing facilities and strengthening of mutual co-operation in the direction of tourism promotion. According to PATA (Pacific Asia Travel Association) tourism directly or indirectly drives more than10% of the world's employment. And if employment will increase than automatically poverty will decrease which may result as decrease in antisocial activities or incidences.

A key element of a successful tourism industry is the ability to recognize and deal with change across a wide range of behavioural and technological factors and the way they interact. In 21st centuary we see the major changes due to shifts in the leisure and tourism environment reflecting changing consumer values, political forces and the explosive growth of information technology. No aspect of industry will remain untouched. These shifts falls in ten principal areas, which together form the New Tourism and Leisure Environment.

Table-10.1. The New Tourism & Leisure Environment..		
Means Turning Away From :	→→	**Turning Towards :**
Old Travel Patterns	→→	New Travel Patterns
Established Destinations	→→	Emerging Destinations
Old Products	→→	New Products
Fragmented Tourism Industry	→→	Economic Development Tool
Developer Control	→→	Community control
Financial Illusion	→→	Financial Reality
Passive Consumers	→→	Involved Participants
Observing Technology	→→	Orchestrating Technology
Mass Markets	→→	Specialty Markets
Mass Marketing→	→→	Direct Customer Communications

In mature markets the trend away from long trip to short breaks has increased the demand for leisure facilities close to source markets. There is also a counter trend towards high yield and extended vacations that are purpose driven by education, wellness, or other forms of programmed self-improvement. The trend toward environment enhancement and heritage protection and anticipation of local people to promote tourism at regional level are the great asset and will be important step in the direction of natural resource management to meet with calamities and disaster and no doubt in this that Spiritual Holiday Eco Tourism will be a great asset to SAARC region.

CHALLENGES

Cross border terrorism, unemployment, poverty, infiltration, cold war, corruption, Law and order condition, poverty are some of the major challenges in the way of tourism growth and co-operation particularly for India, Srilanka, Nepal, Pakistan, Bangladesh. Therefore, these problems require immediate attention from government of concerned country. Important measures should be taken to resolve these issues. Although these problems seem to be complicated but can also be solved by promoting tourism phenomenon and framing suitable strategies and policies with regard to SHET for giving right direction. Tourism has both pushing and pulling factors therefore the aforesaid challenges can be tackled on the basis of common consensus and co-operation. Hence a sound and flexible policy is required to overcome with problems and will help in facing challenges by framing suitable law, rules and regulations in regards to VISA, special permit, custom regulations and other travel formalities.

Only by understanding and acting upon reliable trend forecasts, will the tourism be able to avoid the most common cause of bad decisions, misassumptions about the external demographic, economic, political and technological environment? The growth of travel within the Asia-Pacific region will be both a blessing and a challenge to the industry. There is a new mass tourism 'wave" that is arising from developing Asian economies and less restrictive travel constraints in the region.

IMPACT OF POLICIES

Policy has always been given impacts on the growth and development of tourism as well as people. Right policy can only give the right direction to economic, social and physical development of area whereas wrong policy may result as loss forever. Policy is the mirror of any country in which other country can try to see their face but suppose if mirror is dirty then it will show the dirty face of the concerned country, Hence it should be cleaned and fair having option to change. And also continuous refinement is required for making strong and healthy relationship with neighbor country. New leisure products must be created away from environmentally and culturally sensitive environments because of undesirable impacts and carrying capacity constraints.

The interest and recognition of tourism must take place today; tomorrow may be too late. In most countries, the tourist industry's health is assumed to be the best indicator of a successful policy. This is not so. A tourism policy in a developing nation, particularly, should be judged by its net impact on the economic, social and political life of the people. Since net economic benefits, as opposed to overall receipts and social and political factors are seldom considered quantifiable in many countries they are simply left out of the policy equation.

SUGGESTIVE FRAMEWORK & MODEL

Significant policy initiatives, such as welcoming of private sectors in the country, foreign and NRI investments, setting up of the Tourism Finance Corporation of South Asian Country (TFCSAC for rendering financial assistance & catering to a variety of investors needs of South Asian Countries) and Mutual Co-operation-cum-Investment facilitation cell(should act as a nodal agency that will interact between the investors, the government, the premier financial bodies & the relevant ministries).

Government and non-government agencies should wake up to the need to work closely in partnership on the issue of conservation of environment , forests, coastal areas, tribal belts, hills as well as other flora and fauna.

Guidelines should be framed under which all tourism projects have to get all types of clearance certificate whatsoever reason may be. Today conservationists, economists and tourists alike have awakened to the realization that you can't save nature and monuments at the expense of local people. They are the traditional and time honored custodians of the land and are most likely to lose from conservation and should be convinced that they are the beneficiaries and partners in conservation rather than enemies of it. Therefore Government of these countries should empower the local people and necessary assistance should be provided in terms of money, materials, methods, technology, training & development as well as employment.

International policies and guidelines are required for easy travel formalities and jointly sharing the whole itinerary for getting more benefits out of it. Convenient accessibility for the tourism purposes to be made available for both inbound and outbound tourists. Taxes should be fair enough in all the travelling zones and it should not be a bad dream for tourists.

Unnecessary taxes should be abolished and some common tax policies need to be laid down on the basis of common consensus by organising meeting and conference.

For boosting the civil aviation industry rationalization of Visa procedures is required, Visa should be abolished for visiting the neighboring country as tourist or a lenient Visa requirements should also be drawn up along the procedures.

Establishment of tourism based educational institution, training centres and a Regulatory body to control and monitor the condition of workers, professionals and independent entrepreneurs is required on urgent basis to solve the problems of exploitation and survival.

Political realignment in the South Asian Country particularly for neighboring country of India as free trade zone will encourage travel within each region of SAARC. Reduction in price differential and on branded goods as well as duties and tariff will encourage many forms of travel.

Reasonably safe range of participation is a balance between 30% and 70% for either resident or tourist attendance.

CONCLUSION

Therefore we can say it is time to wake up. We all need to leverage our heritage, the richest tourism potential in the world. We need to leverage nature's enormous gifts to SAARC countries. And we can do it at a very small cost and by making mutual understanding and establishing a long lasting relationship to share the benefits expected to be achieved out of tourism promotion in the region. Several reforms need to incorporate the changing behaviour of tourists in the tourism products and for the implementation of tourism projects on time. Governments of SAARC region need to take initiative to improve the investment climate and policies. Exploitation of workers, professionals must be stopped today by establishing a regulatory body to control and monitor otherwise tomorrow would be too late to overcome with problems.

New travel patterns reflect changes in consumer behaviour, economic strength of source markets, new destinations, and political realignments. Shifts to North-South tourist flows are occurring in Asia (towards ASEAN countries, Australia and the Pacific Islands.) Community interest and tourism must work together for any chance of long term success. In long term, it is not useful to have isolated tourist enclaves. The most rewarding forms of tourism are those that involve both residents and tourists. "Rewarding" means both in terms of the visitor and resident experiences and the economic viability to the developer.

Small business development opportunities, not just jobs, will be an increasingly important element of the community benefit package. The tourism industry should encourage and promote entrepreneurship and privatization particularly at the local level.

REFERENCES

- The Spiritual Tourist: a Personal Odyssey through the Outer Reaches of Belief, Mick Brown (London, Bloomsbury 1999), 310 pp

- Ecotourism and sustainable developments: who owns paradise?, Martha Honey,1999, Business & Economics-405 pages

- South Asia perspectives on Eco-Tourism and conservation, A.P. Krishna, P.D. Rai and J.Subba,2002

- Ethics of tourism development-journal article, Daniel H.Olsen; the Canadian geographer, vol-49, 2005

- Global eco-tourism policies and case studies, Michael Luck and Torsten

Kirstages, Channel view publication,2002.

- International Tourism : Issues and Challenges, D.S. Bhardwaj, Manjula chaudhary; S.S. Boora; Krishna K. Kamra; Ravi Bhushan; Mohinder Chand, Kanishka, 2006,

- Spirituality Affects Performance at work, Article, Ms. Neetu Jain,2006

- Meditation, Acharya Shri Shushil Muni, Article,2007

- Project report "Tourism: Challenges in the new millennium, Chiranjib kumar (2003)

- Dissertation on" Promotion of Buddhist Tourism in Bihar", Chiranjib kumar (2007)

- Travel to India : Yoga & meditation : Popular Destinations (www.india-travel-agents.com)

- www.spiritual.travelmartindia.com)

- www.nextyatra.com/travel

- www.touchskyservices.com

- www.ecotourism.org

- www.tourismindia.com

- www.cii.com

- www.inditravel.com

- www.hrai.com

- www.businessline.com

(Page purposely kept blank)

CHAPTER 11

Day Driving To Reduce Carbon Emission And Pollutions

Controlling the growth rate of carbon emissions and emissions of other toxic gases in the environment has become a mammoth and challenging task for environmentalists, scientists and other conscious people of this world for whom environmental degradation is suicide and equal to genocide. Advancement in transport technology has speedup the economic growth due to excess mobility of people and movement of goods from one place to other but at the same time generated excessive pollution in the air.

The present chapter focuses on the untouched side of environmental conservation techniques by promoting ecotravelling and ecotourism. Day driving is very popular in many countries but it couldn't get recognition throughout the world because it was happening unintentionally more in regards to environment protection. But now it's time to generate awareness regarding its scientific benefits for human beings and environment. The chapter comes out with a suggestive framework of Day Driving for the local government.

INTRODUCTION

Controlling the growth rate of carbon emissions and emissions of other toxic gases in the environment has become a mammoth and challenging task for environmentalists, scientists and other conscious people of this world for whom environmental degradation is suicide and equal to genocide. Globalization and advancement of science and technology has been contributed more negative impacts then positive through production of weapons, missiles, guns, bombs and high speed vehicle with more noise in atmosphere beyond its controls.

Advancement in transport technology has speedup the economic growth due to excess mobility of people and movement of goods from one place to other but at the same time generated excessive pollution in the air. Bus, car, rail, airoplane, and big cruise lines are the best innovative contribution of science and technological development to this world. People can move easily from one destination to other destination in fastest way within an hour or few minutes. At the same time it has provided a huge comfort to travellers, businessmen, professionals and tourists. But the amount of pollution generated by these means of transports is unbearable to nature and its environment. One vehicle (bus, truck, car or bike), vessels (cruise) or air carrier (airoplane) generates almost three types of pollutions i.e. *sound pollution* and *air pollution* directly and *water pollution* directly or indirectly (through toxic rain).

Key Questions are,

Q. Do we think on this issue seriously?

Q. What can be one of the solutions of this problem?

The present paper takes on some issues which are directly and indirectly linked with travelling by means of various transports. It focuses on balancing theory of conservation and protection of environment through human efforts. And those efforts would be successful if, we follow some good and effective principles to improve our lifestyles like "day driving".

DAY DRIVING

It not only saves fuel (energy) but also minimizes chances of loss of life such as human, animals, plants, and other endanger species crossing the road during night and killed due to accident in poor visibility condition. Night has visibility problem always.

Scientifically, during night plants (main producer of oxygen and food) also takes rest, so if, people will drive during night then they will disturb them by light, sound, and carbon emissions. As Sun absent during night so there will be no photosynthesis to evolve fresh oxygen. And it is known that living beings such as animal and plants intakes oxygen in night and releases CO2. So there will be excessive carbon dioxide during night.

Night driving adds more carbon emission to the atmosphere and also it creates disturbance through sound pollution.

Therefore, day driving can be considered as one of the solution of this problem as it would not only decrease the pollution level from the environment but would also boost the tourism business on highway particularly for motels due to more night stay of travellers.

It will also improve the air quality and weather condition in night due to which day will be pleasant.

Country like Ethiopia has day driving system. People says it may be due to some other problem but whatever be the reason, impact of day driving can be seen on environment. Its environment is cleaner than any other country where day driving is not popular. However in some areas pollution is growing due to excessive deforestation and burning of forests for agricultural land and habitat. Even for cooking and other business purposes they are burning wood. But if government will focus on day driving intentionally then it will promote ecotourism with huge employment opportunities and also will clean the environment.

VARIOUS REPORTS ON CARBON EMISSION (some facts)

European Union (EU)--Road transport contributes about one-fifth of the EU's total emissions of carbon dioxide (CO_2), the main greenhouse gas.

Light-duty vehicles – cars and vans – produce around 15% of the EU's emissions of CO_2.

Heavy-Duty Vehicle (HDV)-Trucks, buses and coaches produce about a quarter of CO2 emissions from road transport in the EU and some 5% of the EU's total greenhouse gas emissions – a greater share than international aviation or shipping.

EU legislation requires the greenhouse gas intensity of vehicle fuels to be cut by up to 10% by 2020.

THE CARBON CYCLE

Almost all motor vehicles today burn some kind of "hydrocarbon" fuel be it gasoline, diesel fuel, propane or alcohol. A hydrocarbon is any substance that contains hydrogen and carbon. This includes crude oil, gasoline, diesel fuel, natural gas, coal, wood and even you and me. In other words, hydrocarbons are the chemical building blocks of all living matter past and present. The crude oil we pump from underground today came from ancient peat bogs and forests from millions of years ago -- or so the theory goes.

When anything that contains hydrocarbons is burned, the bonds that bind the hydrogen and carbon atoms together are broken. This releases heat energy, which can then be put to use to power a motor, heat a boiler, cook a meal or whatever. Burning also causes the hydrogen and carbon atoms to combine with oxygen in the air forming water vapour (H_2O) and carbon dioxide (CO_2). That's the basic chemistry of all combustion.

Water vapour is no problem because two-thirds of the Earth's surface is covered with it. So what's a little more? The problem is carbon dioxide. CO_2 is a colorless, odorless, nontoxic, harmless gas. Human beings and animals exhale carbon dioxide with every breath they take. Add to this all the CO_2 that's being produced by every motor vehicle that's being driven, by every furnace that's burning some type of fuel, by every flame that's burning anywhere in the entire world and it adds up to zillions of tons of CO2.

Were it not for plants, we all would have suffocated in our own CO2 a long time ago. Fortunately, plants have the ability to absorb CO2 from the atmosphere and convert it back into organic carbon compounds (hydrocarbons) that become part of the plant. The process requires sunlight and is called "photosynthesis." At the same time, plants release oxygen back into the atmosphere, which we can then use to breathe and burn up more hydrocarbons.

Historically, the amount of naturally occurring CO2 in the atmosphere has been 290 parts per million (only 0.0003%). Air is mostly nitrogen (78%) and oxygen (21%). CO2 is not a pollutant in the traditional sense, but it does retain heat in the Earth's atmosphere. That's why scientists refer to CO2 as a "greenhouse gas." It traps and holds heat just like the glass in a greenhouse.

Based on analysis of air bubbles trapped in ice cores taken at the north and south poles, scientists say the level of CO2 has been gradually rising since the dawn of the Industrial Revolution in the 1700s. When people started burning wood and coal to fuel industrial steam engines and heat their homes, CO2 levels started to rise and have been going up ever since. And since World War II, the rate of increase has been accelerating at an ever quickening pace. The latest count puts CO2 at over 360 parts per million (about a 25% increase).

As CO2 levels continue to rise, scientists fear it will cause a gradual warming of the Earth's average temperature -- which they say has already gone up almost a couple of degrees based on historical data. This, they say, has the potential to upset ocean currents, global weather patterns and rainfall -- which may have far reaching and negative consequences for agriculture, fishing and life in general. Some fear it may even lead to a melting of the polar ice caps causing the oceans to rise and flood coastal areas.

KYOTO PROTOCOL

Concerns over such dire predictions lead to a world summit meeting in Kyoto, Japan in December, 1997. The outcome of this meeting was a proclamation calling for significant reductions in CO_2 emissions by industrialized nations as well as developing nations. The Kyoto Protocol, as it was called, has yet to be finalized.

To reduce CO_2 emissions from cars, we would have to drive smaller, more fuel efficient cars, raise the fuel economy requirements for trucks, and adopt a variety of conservation measures to reduce energy consumption.

SUVS VERSUS TREES

If cars and trucks put carbon dioxide into the atmosphere and trees remove it, how many trees does it take to offset the carbon released by one sport utility vehicle?

One gallon of gasoline weighs about 6.2 lbs. Of that, over 5 lbs. is carbon (the rest is hydrogen). According to the EPA, burning one gallon of gasoline produces about 19.4 pounds of carbon dioxide (CO_2).

If a SUV that gets 15 mpg is driven 15,000 miles a year, it will burn 1,000 gallons of gas. That puts about 19,400 lbs. of carbon into the atmosphere (combined with oxygen as CO_2).

A mature tree 40 to 50 feet high weighs around 10,000 lbs. Of that, at least 7,000 lbs. is organic carbon compounds (the exact amount will vary depending on the species and the density of the wood). To reach this size, most trees need 30 to 40 years of growing time. This too will vary depending on the species of tree, its geographical location, soil conditions and weather. Trees in hot, wet tropical climates grow a lot faster than trees in northern climates.

Assuming these estimates are reasonably accurate, one to two mature trees contains about as much carbon as the gasoline burned by a typical SUV in a year.

But remember it takes 30 to 40 years for the tree to absorb all that carbon from the atmosphere. The process of "photosynthesis" takes time. Leaves use sunlight and water to convert CO_2 from the atmosphere into sugar that the tree uses to grow and build more wood fibre. The tree's average carbon uptake, therefore, may only be about 200 lbs. of carbon a year.

To offset the carbon released by driving a SUV 15,000 mile a year, therefore, it takes at least 35 medium-sized healthy trees to convert CO_2 into wood.

What happens to the carbon once it's been taken out of the atmosphere by the trees and bound up in the wood? It stays there until something happens to the tree.

But if the tree is destroyed in a forest fire, is burned to clear land or is cut for firewood, all of the carbon that's been stored in the tree since it was a sapling is immediately released back into the atmosphere as CO_2. Consequently, burning a tree is the carbon equivalent of driving a gas-guzzling SUV for a year

UPGRADATION OF GREEN TECHNOLOGY IN VEHICLES

Clean and green technological upgradation in vehicles, air carriers and cruise liners would ofcourse improve the air quality of atmosphere but following eco-friendly principles like Ecotravelling, eco-business and ecotourism will not only decreases the percentage of hazard gases but would also be able to sustain in long term as such principles generate more awareness among people and follows the sustainable development concept. We should never forget here that " prevention is better than cure". Therefore instead of focussing on new type of vehicle like electric, solar, battery or something else, it's better to look into the "Day Driving" concept and its implementation as policy to improve our environment.

The following charts tells about the
ncreasing rate of carbon emissions
in the world,

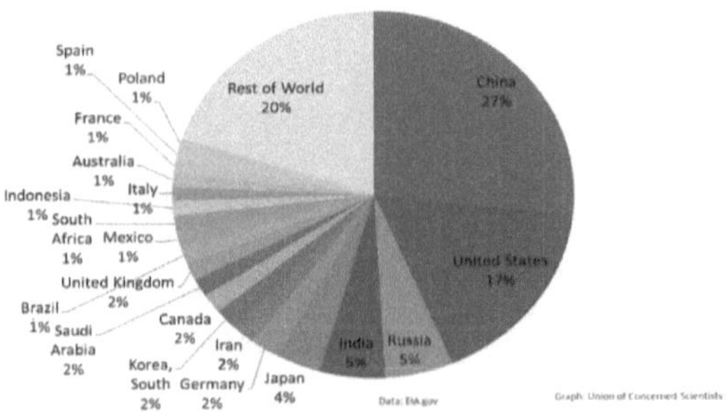

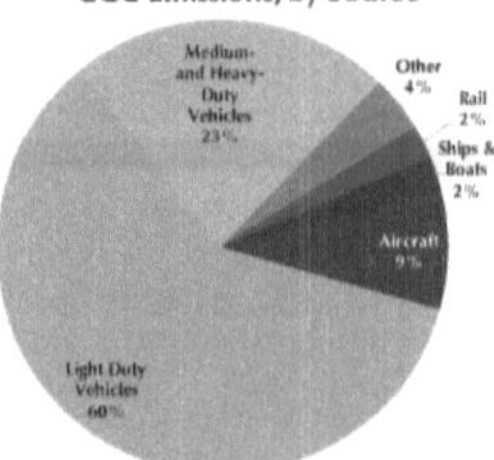

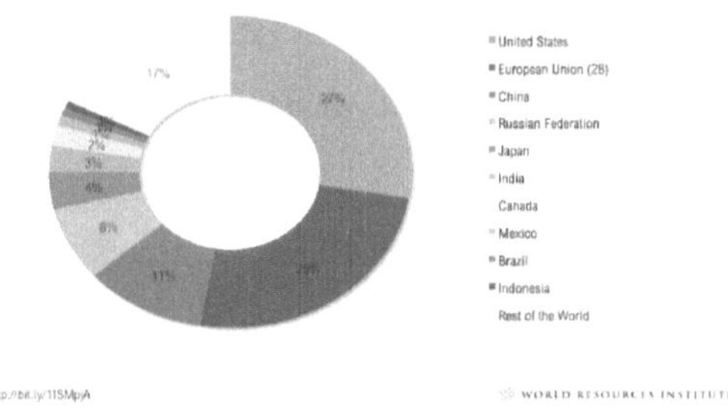

SUGGESTIVE FRAMEWORK -

(i) Day Driving Only: Driving during day time only and taking rest in night at some roadside/highway motels.

(ii) No Night Driving (except in some emergency cases or urgent need).

(iii) Minimum Use of Horn- plants and some species are very sensitive to sound. It may kill them also or it may even result in fall of big trees. Various researches in science have already proved it.

(iv)No Overloading- overloading from carrying capacity is hazardous for both soil and atmosphere. Over Loaded vehicles produce more sound, more carbons and consume more fuels at the same time it exerts more pressure on earth's upper surface and breaks the structure.

(v) Planting at least 10 trees after every 2000 kilometers of driving and getting certificate of plantation from certified authority (town/village municipal commission) or block/district agricultural /horticulture department.

(vi) Insisting others also to follow the same principle(day driving) or else keeping distant from such people.

(v) First priority is to establish "Day Driving & Ecotravelling Cell" or in every village/town/ district /country for the verification, vigilance of driving and also issuing of "Ecotraveller Certificate" to the people follow the principle. This cell will give reward to ecotraveller and punishment (to plant 30 trees or contribute to natures conservation activities) to law breaker (regular travellers).

(vi) Membership scheme for all travel and tour operators and benefits in tax holiday involving them through various environmental conservation activities.

(vii) Separate schemes and benefits for industrial logistic and supply chain department for following the day driving and no-overloading principles. Schemes may be tax subsidy or other way incentives.

(vii) Involving different NGOs at local level to monitor and facilitate the smooth day driving process.

(ix) Deputing Highway Patrolling Police, Airlines Traffic Controllers or

Airport Managers, Cruise Line Operators or Harbour Masters for such type of monitoring and evaluation jobs.

(X) Cruise liners may go for night fleet also as it has to travel through dense water most of the time and sometime due to uncontrollable circumstances such as tides, storm etc. it becomes difficult to reach to nearest mainland area. And anchoring in dense see during night is dangerous.

(xi) Airlines may be allowed to fly in night hours as it fly at very high altitude but again generates more pollution in the air so to compensate it they have to plant more trees on ground and has to take care for zero pollution on ground handling system.

(xii) Individual and Independent Membership schemes for the people driving their own vehicles personally. They may be rewarded or promoted as an ambassador of "Day Driving Eco-travellers" . Here we need to redesign the concept of ecotourism and ecotravelling.

(xiii) Eco-motel concept need to be developed and motels following the norms of ecotels and sustainable development should be given the status of "eco-motels" and incentives or tax benefits must be given to them with award.

(xiv) Best Day Driving Destination trophy - need to be given to the local authority and local people together for their rigorous efforts and contribution to clean and green environment through day driving.

Note: With fewer trees left to absorb carbon and more vehicles producing carbon, don't expect the atmosphere's carbon balance to improve any time soon.

SOME IMPORTANT TERMS

Ecotourism: "Responsible travel to natural areas that conserves the environment and improves the well-being of local people." The International Ecotourism Society(TIES, 1990) Principles of Ecotourism: Ecotourism is about uniting conservation, communities, and sustainable travel. This means that those who implement and participate in ecotourism activities should follow the following Eco-tourism principles: Minimize impact. •Build environmental and cultural awareness and respect. •Provide positive experiences for both visitors and hosts. •Provide direct financial benefits for conservation. •Provide financial benefits and empowerment for local people. •Raise sensitivity to host countries' political, environmental, and social climate

Ecotraveller/ Ecotourist-more educated than other tourists, with an interest in learning about the environment. Eco-tourists tend to travel all year round and are not as seasonally biased. Preferred ecofriendly vehicles most of the time and more likely to be involved in pro-environmental behavior at home such as recycling household waste; purchasing green products; many of them belong to conservation organizations; but are not necessarily active in them- having a more intellectual interest in the environment rather than hands-on experience . Accommodation Preferences–More interested in specialist accommodation in a natural and ecofriendly setting than traditional star rated hotels.

CONCLUSION

Day driving can be considered as important principles through which carbon emissions and emission of other gases minimized. Many countries have been following day driving system since a long time intentionally or unintentionally. But it's time now to think it intentionally and innovatively. Global warming is growing challenge for everyone. It may help upto certain extent. It may not be acceptable for many countries particularly for developing countries as it will decrease the level of mobility of people, goods and services which will give impact on economic growth. But still we need to think on the line of sustainability and sustainable development. And it demands little sacrifice to conserve scarce resources. Initially it may not give very good result but in long term it would be excellent.

REFERENCES

- Aditi C, Kumar C., 2015, Ecotourism Planning Development & Marketing, Bharti Publication, New Delhi

- Chiranjib K.,2016, Day driving to control carbon emission perspective of Ecotourism, International Journal of Scientific Research, Volume : 5, Issue : 4

- https://www3.epa.gov/climate change/ghgemissions/global.h tml

- http://www.c2es.org/federal/e xecutive/vehicle-standards

- http://www.aa1car.com/librar y/co2.htm

- http://www.ucsusa.org/global _warming/science_and_impact s/science/each-countrys-share-of-co2.html

- http://ec.europa.eu/clima/pol
  icies/transport/vehicles/index
  _en.htm

- http://www.wri.org/blog/2014
  /11/6-graphs-explain-
  world%E2%80%99s-top-10-
  emitters

****

(page purposely left blank)

CHAPTER 12

Mountaineering Tourism : Future Revival Plan

Abstract

Corona (Covid19) pandemic has posed a big challenge on mountaineering tourism operators. The present article focuses on the various dimensions and revival plan for the mountaineering tourism in wider aspect to grab upcoming opportunities from the market. Mountain tourism need to be expanded to mountaineering tourism beyond the image of adventure tourism only.

Key words: Corona(Covid19),Mountaineering, Mountain tourism, Revival, Tour Operator

1. Introduction

Mountaineering tourism has been emerged as one of the eco-friendly tourism product in the world. But to retain its potential to attract different types of tourists, Destination Management Organisations (DMO) need to explore taped and untapped tourism resources. Tourism has been a worst hit sector after Corona(Covid19) outbreak.

The corona(Covid19) pandemic has turned tourism into new dimension which is going to open the doors of new opportunities for tour operators and tourists. People will take lessons from such pandemic and would plan their tourism destination on the basis of availability of health safety, natural attractions, wildlife and organic food items as well as distance from home. The unexpected decrease in annual family income due to economy slowdown; job insecurity, health hazards and safety; and other contingency will affect the selection of tourism destination. Eco-friendly destinations having potential to provide organic food and tourism activities in natural setting would be remained in high demand.

Mountaineering tourism has tremendous potential to grab the opportunity through nature based tourism. It could be emerged as an important tourism product but need to be redefined and redesigned to offer ultimate satisfaction among visitors, tourists and guests. A good product mix could help in grabbing opportunity from the new emerging market.

2. Revival Plan

The following points would be helpful in revival of mountaineering tourism,

I. Mountaineering Tourism should not be considered as type of adventure tourism only.
II. Mountaineering needs to be divided into the culture, food, farm, leisure and health.
III. Wildlife tourism needs to be treated as one of the important variable to retain the tourists for longer duration.
IV. Birds watching, Orchid trekking and animal safari would have potential to attract.
V. Visit to cultural village located in the mountains and participating in ethnic food preparation and cultural dance.
VI. Closing of all types of "Wet Market" in the locality and generating awareness.
VII. Highlighting closure of all types of "Wet Markets" in the promotional campaign or advertisements.
VIII. Designing teasers and trailers in combination of more than two types of tourism products.
IX. Designing tourism/tour programs metrics in combination format.

X. Focus should be given on Ecotourism programs and responsible tourism.

XI. Developing Recreation Opportunity Spectrum(ROS) as per carrying capacity and limits of acceptable change in destination.

XII. Authenticity and originality of destination should not be transformed completely in any case.

XIII. Designing tour packages by involving tourists for generating learning experiences and awareness regarding nature and culture.

XIV. Biodiversity conservation to be kept on priority.

XV. Tax holiday for tour operator, travel agencies and ecolodge owners if they involve local community to provide their services.

XVI. Devoping cooperative system and schemes to promote indigenous cultural and agricultural products.

XVII. *Community Based Tourism Programme* and *Event Book system* would be of great help in monitoring of natural resources and conservation.

XVIII. Wildlife trekking (trekking of wild animals and plants) & Caving.

XIX. Developing family package considering product bundling means opportunity for all. Paying attention at individual level while designing various activities in the package.

XX. Promoting tourism through regional cooperation.

XXI. Mountaineering Tourism need to be converted into Mountain Tourism in terms of getting wider publicity and scope.

XXII. Targeting domestic and regional market.

XXIII. Setting up local financial cooperation to facilitate financial assistance for new start-up.

XXIV. Listing of tourism programs in the brochure and websites of educational institutions and corporate houses located in plain areas (at low altitude).

XXV. Arranging demo activities and video presentation on Mountain Tourism in collaboration with tour operators in various educational institutions and industries.

XXVI. Listing of new geomorphological sites with ecological and health benefits.

XXVII. Inviting students and parents for various competition/challenge on mountaineering and mountain tourism and providing them with reward/award to the winner.

XXVIII. Telecasting such programs(tourism competitions/challenge) on YouTube, Facebook, Instagram, LinkedIn and other TV channels to attract.

XXIX. Tie up with international mountaineering tourism organizations, tour Operators like,

- ➢ Butterfield and Robinson (Bike Trips/ Mountain Biking)
- ➢ Abercrombie and Kent (trekking, Everest)
- ➢ Harvesham and Baker Golfing Expedition (Golf)
- ➢ MICATO Safari
- ➢ While Journey (Ethnic Food and culture)
- ➢ World Culture Tour
- ➢ Martin Randall Travel

3. Recommendations

Golf course could be developed to attract sports tourism as major activities. Mountain Sport Tourism(MST) has also a wider scope in future.

- Capacity building programmes, woman empowerment and youth guide training program would help in achieving sustainable development goals in regards to Mountain Tourism.
- Involving local community in production of services would decrease the labour cost and overhead cost which will further help in

discounted pricing strategy of various tour packages.
- Soft adventure programs need to be designed and promoted.
- Highlights of health safety measure and tourist-host awareness through various promotional tools would develop trust among tourists.
- Promoting *Travel Health Insurance*(THI) to tourists at nominal charge would add more benefits to product.
- Taking guidance/consultancy from specialist of areas like professor/ research scholar s/ tour operators, frequent visitors and other tourism professionals

4. **Limitations of existing study** : any generalized idea is not right due to variations in size, goal, changing perceptions and region and literatures followed.

Further Reading (Books)

- https://www.amazon.com/Ecotourism-Dynamics-Perspective-Wildlife-Dimensions/dp/1546833447/

- https://www.amazon.com/Ecotourism-Planning-Development-Marketing-Chiranjib/dp/1539170691/

- https://www.tourismjournals.asia/Articles-/-Insight/

****More books on** www.ckihmt.com

(page purposely left blank)